COLDPLAY
Look at the Stars

COLDPLAY
Look at the Stars

Gary Spivack

POCKET BOOKS   **booKs**

New York | London | Toronto | Sydney

POCKET BOOKS · MTV BOOKS

POCKET BOOKS, a division of Simon & Schuster, Inc.
1230 Avenue of the Americas, New York, NY 10020

Copyright © 2004 by Gary Spivack

MTV Music Television and all related titles, logos, and
characters are trademarks of MTV Networks, a division
of Viacom International Inc.

ISBN: 0-7434-9196-3

First MTV Books/Pocket Books trade paperback edition
July 2004

10 9 8 7 6 5 4 3 2 1

Photo credits: Kevin Westenberg: viii–1, 2, 5, 12, 56, 84, 97,
124, 130, 134; Jay Blakesberg: 8, 14, 16, 25, 29, 33, 36–37,
42, 46–47, 58–59, 63, 75, 86 (L), 92–93, 98–99, 107, 108,
122, 123, 129(L); Jeff Kravitz: 30, 38, 41, 52, 55, 71, 73,
105, 113(L); Stephen Lovekin/FilmMagic: 6, 21, 22, 66, 76;
Mark Henderson/Retna UK: 11; Kevin Mazur/WireImage: 27;
Lester Cohen/WireImage: 39, 45, 110, 113(R); Leo Gozbekian:
68; Gozbekian Photographers: 72; Soren McCarty/WireImage:
83; Mike Guastella/WireImage: 86(R); Steve Granitz/WireImage:
87; Tim Jackson/WireImage: 88; Michael Caulfield/WireImage:
114–115, 116, 119; Diena/Brengola/WireImage: 120;
Kevin Kane/WireImage: 129(R); courtesy of the author: 136.

Manufactured in the United States of America

For information regarding special discounts for bulk
purchases, please contact Simon & Schuster Special Sales
at 1-800-456-6798 or business@simonandschuster.com

Design: Office In Concept

This book is dedicated to my children, Jake and Emma . . . living proof, guys, that dreams really can become realities. They can, but only if you are willing to put in the hard work and passion (throw in a bit of luck, too) that it takes to make your dreams come true.

Contents

Guy Berryman
Bass

Will Champion
Drums

Chris Martin
Lead vocals, piano,
rhythm guitar

Jonny Buckland
Lead guitar

Coldplay: Look at the Stars
Gary Spivack

Introduction

"Nobody Said It Was Easy"

Coldplay's multiple personalities. Coldplay's ever changing moods. To even attempt to define this rock band with one expression, one adjective, or even one sentence would be an exercise in futility. This is Coldplay's charm; their power. The contradictions that exist 24/7 with Coldplay are as simple as one sentence, one thought, that can spontaneously come out of Coldplay's front man Chris Martin's mouth. While backstage, at yet another sold-out show during one of the six legs of their continuous 2002–2003 North American trek, Martin casually blurts out, "We are the best band in the world, but I just wish my hair wasn't falling out," immediately followed by, "We have the best job possible. I know we work hard, but I feel so guilty that we are so adored for what we do." The paradox of Coldplay is their magic. Confident but insecure. Ambitious but humble. Friendly but moody (see Chris Martin). Precise but unpredictable. Self-doubting but self-assured. When informed by *Spin* magazine that they were named Band of the Year for 2003, Martin's response was, "Thanks very much. So . . . is this going to be a story about how you've named us Band of the Year, but take it back because we don't really deserve it?" It's this constant tug of war that makes this four-piece outfit, made up of best friends that met in college, tick. It's these "Sybil-like" qualities that help to make Coldplay stand alone.

Coldplay is four distinct personalities from the four corners of England who quickly became best mates. They all lived in the same freshman dormitory, Ramsey Hall at UCL, University of London. For the love of music and friendship, they formed a band and started a union together that would share the same vision, the same goals, and same ambitions.

This is a tale that you have heard and have seen countless times. But what makes this rock band different from the countless others on the endless rock 'n' roll conveyor belt? What makes them different from 99 percent of all other bands trying to get their small sliver of the rock pie?

And, of course, what has made Coldplay the world's most vital, urgent, and pivotal rock band in this new century?

Coldplay is a cut above the norm . . . no question. And Coldplay refuses to be labeled, cramped, compromised, or confined. There's a constant push and pull that exists between their public perception and their inner private circle, a circle that doesn't allow strangers or intruders. This give and take jerks at the root of the band and clearly at the heart of their charismatic lead singer. In the same *Spin* article that awarded them with Band of the Year honors, Martin says, "Every front man is a mixture of insecurity and confidence . . . of wanting to be private, but also to have thousands of people clapping every night. I'm constantly confused by it." The constant struggle between what is right for Coldplay's soul and what is right for Coldplay's wallet brings with it a sense of responsibility that most bands could not carry. They have passed on countless offers and opportunities from advertising agencies, TV networks, and movie companies to license their music. In one fifteen-minute span, in a band meeting backstage before a concert in Milwaukee, manager Dave Holmes informed the band of offers from a car company, an American beverage company, and even an underwear company; the band passed on all, leaving more than a cool million on the table. This was happening on a weekly, if not daily, basis for Coldplay. In the same meeting, Holmes told the band that they had been invited to perform on the 2003 MTV Music Awards show. Holmes thought it would be a grand idea to use that show as a launch date for a thirty-show tour that would touch upon every key market in the United States. The band stood its ground,

claiming burnout and overexposure, and citing the potential damage to their long-term goals. The band won this battle, settling on doing just the VMAs, sacrificing well over $500,000 per member. The continuing attempt of being pulled down the river of rock 'n' roll clichés has made these four young, middle-class, and university-educated Englishmen grow . . . and grow up. All in their early to mid-twenties, Chris, Jonny, Guy, and Wil have become old souls . . . quickly.

"Nobody said it was easy. Nobody said it would be this hard. Let's take it back to the start." —"The Scientist"

I want us to be the biggest, best band in the fucking world and we're gonna keep trying and trying until we get there. [Chris Martin]

Backstage, only minutes from show time, it seemed like just another evening on tour for the four members of Coldplay. Bass player Guy Berryman was in the hallway near the main dressing room kicking a soccer ball to himself. Jonny Buckland, lead guitarist, was casually sitting on one of the dressing room couches, calmly strumming an unplugged electric guitar. Wil Champion, drummer, could be seen either playing one of the band's many video games in a side room or quietly dribbling his basketball (yes, an Englishman who loves basketball!). And Chris Martin, Coldplay's public face and lead singer, had already begun his nightly routine of vocal warm-ups (imagine a veteran-sounding opera singer warming up before a show) in one of the many private shower stalls that occupy the backstage area. For those in Coldplay's circle everything

was status quo, just your normal preshow rituals. Here they were, about to jump on the most famous of rock 'n' roll stages in arguably the most important city for a rock 'n' roll band and they were proceeding unfazed, without any noticeable signs of fear. This is part of Coldplay's beauty . . . their mystique. Nothing seems to rattle these guys. They have the confidence of a Michael Jordan game-winning jumper. Yes, they knew where they were . . . they knew exactly where they were. "It's great to play places of historical significance like the Hollywood Bowl, Red Rocks, or Madison Square Garden where our favorite bands have played," Champion calmly states. The Rolling Stones, Led Zeppelin, Bruce Springsteen, the Police, U2, Radiohead to name but a few, and now it was Coldplay's turn to join the ranks of the elite that have headlined New York City's most treasured rock 'n' roll venue.

In just under three years, Coldplay had criss-crossed North America nine times (six in support of *A Rush of Blood to the Head* alone); a rather impressive resume in such a short span. This was actually the second time they graced the Garden stage, having performed on the 2002 Grammy Awards. But now they returned to America's premiere venue to headline their own show, having become the anointed ones . . . the chosen. They took on America, with history and conventional rule against them, and came out victorious.

Not quite the way it was for Coldplay just two years earlier.

"Let's take it back to the start."
—"The Scientist"

Friday, February 16, 2001
Irving Plaza
New York City
Attendance: 1,200 (sold out in 2 hours)

"I'm sorry to say that I'm sick and I don't know how long we can go tonight. Please don't hate us," Chris Martin told the sold-out crowd at New York's City's popular Irving Plaza. This was not a good thing. This was a paramount show for Coldplay, their debut show in New York City; only the most significant city in the most important country for any rock band interested in world domination. News of Coldplay's pulling the plug spread like wildfire. The national college music newspaper *Hear/Say* reported, "In New York City, Coldplay battled through a performance of 'Yellow' during a taping of *Late Night with Conan O'Brien*, but it was clear that Martin was not in great shape. His voice cracked. Nervously, he bit into his acoustic guitar with enough force to break a string. Later that night, the band heroically attempted to pull off the New York gig at Irving Plaza. But it was to no avail. Coldplay pulled out as Martin was simply to sick too continue."

It was February 16, 2001, and the buzz was overwhelming. Tickets were next to impossible to find and fans had been waiting for this show since they first heard the single "Yellow" on the radio, and had seen the accompanying video all over MTV. Coldplay was on a one-way subway to "the next big thing." Backstage, Martin told a reporter from the New York *Daily News* that, "We consider it to be a fluke, but we may have broken through because a lot of people who aren't into heavy metal

aren't being catered to. They're looking for something else." The success of "Yellow" on modern rock radio was a shocker and stunner to many. When the song was in its beginning stages nobody, outside a few brave employees at Capitol Records and a handful of radio programmers, gave Coldplay much of a shot to succeed. Nearly every other song charting at the radio format was recorded by a rap-metal act or leftover alternative grunge band. But now anyone in the music industry who was cool, trying to look cool, or trying to be cool either was at Irving Plaza or claimed to be there. On a cold and stormy winter night (typical), this was clearly the hottest ticket in town. And the band's leader, Chris Martin, wanted nothing to do with it.

"Why should we care about America? Why should we put in the effort? All our favorite bands come over to America and fail. Why is our little band going to be any different?" Those were the very first words out of Martin's mouth when their newly appointed comanager Dave Holmes flew overseas to meet Coldplay for the first time in the summer of 2000. "They had watched bands such as the Stone Roses, the Verve, the Charlatans and, the Manic Street Preachers . . . huge arena-sized bands in their home country . . . come over to the States and just flop. Stories of playing in front of half-filled clubs, while back home they all play in front of ten thousand-plus fans, really put Coldplay on the defense," claims Holmes.

The whole day in New York was a nightmare. Coldplay had what is known as a "promo day from hell." A meeting at MTV to shake the hands of executives, a radio interview at the preeminent WXRK-FM , who gave them a grand total of five precious minutes of air time because "Yellow" was the only song the station played from the band (standard practice for any developing act on a major market radio station), a rushed but all-important national TV appearance on *Late Night with Conan O'Brien*, and back to more "grips and grins" with music executive types at an industry dinner put together by Capitol. Imagine a dinner where you are the guest of honor and you have no idea who the twenty people seated at your table are. Most of the music executives were there because it was a chance to have a free meal and cocktails on Capitol's dime and by this time no band member was in any kind of mood to strike up a conversation with a total stranger. Then, after all that and fighting one hell of a nasty flu, there was this sold-out concert to deal with. Martin recalled that day for *CMJ Music Monthly*. "I hated it. I just wanted to play. All this promotion just causes stress and worry. When we have to do all this talking about music, it depresses us. I know that as soon as we get back in the rehearsal room, we'll be like, 'Oh yeah, this is what we love.' "

This is so great . . . what we do. Our job is so ridiculously great. I think about that all the time. Someone must have bribed someone along the way; to that person who did the bribing on our behalf, thanks a lot. [Chris Martin]

The house lights went down and the buzzing crowd greeted the four young Englishmen with the warmth of seeing old friends for the first time in years. It wouldn't last long. After Martin's disclaimer about how under the weather he was, he launched into the hypnotizing ballad "Trouble." The crowd knew

something wasn't right. There was a real labor and tightness to Martin's performance, the kind of labor that one witnesses when watching a teenager murder his own piano recital. "After the first song, Chris asked if anyone in the crowd knew the words to 'Yellow.' Many in the front immediately raised their hands and he picked this extremely over-weight girl to join the band onstage," says Mike Parrish, VP/Operations at trade magazine *FMQB*. "Coldplay went into 'Yellow' and this girl just destroyed the song. Her saving grace was that she knew the words to the song; but, aside from that, it just totally sucked." The band got through "Yellow" and, one by one, the four members of Coldplay made their way off the stage. That was it. House lights on, two songs in, show over . . . game over. The New York media recorded the sad truth. "Coldplay was poised to make its biggest splash yet, with a small but high-profile date at Irving Plaza. It didn't happen. Wracked with a whopper of a winter cold, lead singer Chris Martin did one song, tried karaoke on another, and promptly canceled the rest of the gig," reported the *New York Post*. *The New York Times* made it national news. "Coldplay is a band to watch. Not just because they are a talented band on its way up, but also because at any moment they might implode. . . . Here's hoping Coldplay will survive to release a sophomore album." Quite a mark to leave on America's most prominent city.

"Yellow," the first stateside single, was flying up the modern rock charts with every major station in the country running the song in high rotation. The video to "Yellow," a spectacular one-camera shot that follows Martin along a beach on a typically dreary day in England, had been deemed "buzzworthy" by MTV and was clocking significant air-time. *Parachutes* was ascending the album charts. This band was making real strides in the States, but if you were witness to the ill-fated Irving Plaza show on February 16th, then you would have only imagined the opposite to be true.

From there, the much talked about, highly antici-pated first American tour for Coldplay was history. The rest of the tour, about five cities, was canceled, and like their peers before them (the Verve, Blur, Manic Street Preachers, etc.) Coldplay went back home with their tails between their legs. "We couldn't hold it together. Chris was fed up. He couldn't sing a whole gig anymore, and this had never happened to us," remembers Buckland. "If you watch a tape of that *Conan* performance you can see the stress he was under and hear the strain in his voice." Wil Champion chimes in: "It was the dead of winter, we all had bad colds, all tired, stressed, and homesick. Chris's voice went out early in the tour, due to the constant promo we were doing, and we just wanted it to stop."

"On that first tour, I recall flying from San Francisco to Boston or something and it was like a six-hour flight. I just remember landing and saying, 'Fuck . . . we're still in America?' You fly six hours in Europe and you've crossed like six countries," laughs Buckland.

"When we got home, my dad pulled me aside and said I've got to treat this more like a boxing match. You get hit, you get up. If you fall down, you make damn sure you get up again. Keep on fighting. Words to live by," preaches Martin. Where what happened at Irving Plaza would have scared away

most bands, this only fueled the fire for Chris, Jonny, Guy, and Wil. Coldplay had already estab-lished themselves as a force in England, Ireland, Scotland, Austrailia, and New Zealand. America was big, very big, and it was the nineteenth country on their various passports in less than a year. But when they all boarded the airplane at JFK to return home, they didn't have the feeling they'd be back anytime soon.

The self-doubt, the minute-to-minute angst, the insecurity, the stress all seemed to pour out in a flood on their dreadful first trip to the States. In the end, Martin and company could only *"blame it upon a rush of blood to the head."*

Chapter 2

"Look at the Stars/Look How They Shine on You"

No fucking way. No way in hell a band from "across the pond" is going to get played on American modern rock radio in the year 2000. Not in this environment. This was my and several of my contemporaries' feelings. In the summer of 2000, I was the VP/Promotion at Capitol Records in Hollywood. In charge of all promotion and marketing efforts for rock and alternative music on the label's current and active roster, my primary responsibility was to get airplay, to get these bands, (good, bad, or pure shit) played *on the radio*.

That summer, America's modern rock radio stations were dominated by mosh pit-charged anthems from artists like Limp Bizkit, Marilyn Manson, Nine Inch Nails, Korn, and Godsmack. Hey, at least there was Rage Against the Machine. Manufactured anger, get your angst at the local minimall, muscle rock was at an all-time high. Testosterone levels were peaking at radio stations. As Gary Susman of the *Boston Phoenix* put it, "On American radio, it's 1963 again. There's plenty of immaculately produced teen pop, but rock 'n' roll is as good as dead. A band such as Coldplay faces an uphill battle against the overwhelming American indifference to British rock. By the end of the nineties, hip-hop and homegrown alternative rock ruled the radio.

Listeners in the States couldn't be bothered to discover British rock." Radio station research and overall response that programmers were getting back from their audience was siding with this theory. "What our listeners wanted during this time was hard, loud, and in-your-face rock music. All kinds of popular music has its cycles and it was just hard rock's turn at the wheel. My core listeners couldn't get enough of it," explains WBCN program director Oedipus. Simply put, there was little room for a band of Coldplay's compassionate manner and sensitivity to be found on American rock radio. And what's impossible to avoid, the front man in this band plays the piano! To top it off . . . they are from England. England's batting average in the United States was at the bottom with no sign of recovery. Oasis and their continued antics had already muddied the waters for everyone else trying to come over from the UK. Blur and their follow-up to "Song 2," a big modern rock staple only two years before, was a disaster. Even Robbie Williams, who was signed to Capitol Records in America no less, the ten-times-over platinum artist of the Great Britain pop world, barely reached gold record status (sales of 500,000 records) in the States.

". . . and it's called 'Yellow.' " Those were the first lines that I couldn't get out of my head when I first heard Coldplay's music. I didn't know it at the time, but I was listening to an import copy of a song called "Yellow" by a new band signed by our sister company EMI/Parlaphone out of the UK. The song was coming through the office walls of Capitol Record's College Radio Promotion department. I shared a wall with their office and on a daily basis would constantly hear unfamiliar music emanating from their side of the wall. I rarely, if ever, gave it a second thought; most of the music they played would go in one ear and out the other. Frankly, the music that came out of that office was nothing more than good, old-fashioned art rock bullshit. You know the type—the too-cool-for-school college rock. Off-key vocals, badly tuned guitars with percussion that sounded as if the drummer were playing his kit in a bathtub filled with water. But this time it was different.

"What is that?" I asked as I stood in their door. "It's an import. Band is called Coldplay. They're about to be huge in England," said one of the many interns that come in and out of that office. I asked to borrow the one copy they had so I could listen to it on my drive home. For the fifty minutes it took me to get from Capitol to my home in West Los Angeles I was hooked. For once, the traffic I fought every night didn't faze me. Lush, romantic, sensitive, hypnotic, dreamy, swirling, stunning, beautiful, infectious; these are some of the words to describe what I heard when I first listened to such tracks as "Spies," "Shiver," "Everything's Not Lost," "Don't Panic," and "Yellow." Great . . . just great, I thought. In the year 2000, words like "beautiful," "romantic," and "dreamy" were nails in the coffin to modern rock radio programmers. I personally loved it, and it was like the clouds above had just parted, but for American rock radio to actually "play" this . . . no fucking way.

If anything, there was room for one and only one. And that was Radiohead. To Capitol Records, September 2000 was all about Radiohead and the imminent release of *Kid A*. *Kid A* was everything Capitol had hoped for, debuting as it did at number 1 on *Billboard's* album chart the week of September

18th with sales of over 200,000! *Number 1? What? Has anyone really listened to* Kid A*? Like, all the way through?* One could argue that it is the most bizarre number 1 record in the history of the charts. The album featured the song "Optimistic" that made it all the way to the Top 10 on the modern rock chart. An incredible feat considering the lay of the land; Kid Rock was belting out "Bawitdaba." "Optimistic," at its peak, became the perfect "flavor" track for any station that played guitar-based rock. Getting a song like "Optimistic" and a band like Radiohead up and over on American radio was a monumental victory. At the time, you got the sense there was finally a light at the end of the tunnel, that there was hope that something other than recycled rap rock could cut through on rock radio.

We're not a sports-metal band. We don't scream or play out of tune. If you like a band that is passionate about writing great songs and really meaning it when they sing it, then we'll be your favorite band. [Chris Martin]

Kid A cracked the door open . It was a small crack, but enough to let four reserved young Englishmen known as Coldplay slip through. Once in, they kicked the door wide open. With *Kid A* now platinum and the envy of the entire music industry, Capitol Records had a new wave of, well . . . optimism. *Can it be done again? Can another band from "across the pond" achieve success in America? Is there room for two?* Maybe, just maybe, the world was indeed waiting, desperately waiting for "a Coldplay" to come along and, well . . . along came Coldplay.

"We immediately bonded. We all were influenced by music that is soulful and emotive. It was rather obvious that we were all going to be mates," recalls Champion. For the first time in their young lives, each one was away from the comfort of their parents' homes and this only brought them closer.

Martin looks back. "It started in 1996. We were friends for about a year before we started playing and writing songs. It's like finding a wife. It's great to know your wife as a friend first or whatever, then when you get together you already know each other. That's what happened with us. By the time we actually started playing music, we were already best of friends." Martin and Buckland even took jobs as janitors in the dormitory to help support themselves and pay for the musical equipment they needed to perform live. Once the band became the collective priority, their unique democratic writing process took hold. To this day, they have never strayed from the system they created all the way back in 1996. "I'd come in with a riff or a melody and that's where the production line begins; like an assembly line at a factory," Martin explains. "It's always what they put on that makes it, to me, special. 'Cause I was writing on my own since I was eleven, and the songs were always just okay, but without the other three, the songs would be nothing. Without any one of the four of us, it would be a total waste of time."

Chris and Jonny were the first to pair up and take a crack at creating original material. "There was no plan B," recalls Martin, "Meeting Jonny was like falling in love. With Jonny, I started to get more of a musical education; things like Jeff Buckley and Radiohead." They started writing songs together with dorm neighbor Guy, who joined on the bass shortly after. Wil, who had arranged an audition for his roommate to drum with the three, ended up joining after his roomie flaked on the audition "Thank God we got Wil to join the band, 'cause we had some hard luck with drummers. The drummer before him was just . . . loopy," explains Martin. "We just hacked about really, but there was like this immediate chemistry, ya know . . . I can't really describe it, but it was there and we all knew it. Right from the start, Jonny and I sat down and wrote this song called 'Love I'm So Tired'. He had this chord sequence and I started writing, and I found myself singing cooler things than I'd ever sung before." The four shared a clear and burning passion for music and a commitment to be serious about the new art they were making. They rehearsed everywhere and anywhere they could, one anothers' dorm rooms, bathrooms, basements, and even public parks. "We would head up to Jonny's room after lectures to rehearse," remembers Champion. "It wasn't a big room at all. There'd be a ton of amplifiers around the place. We had to cover the drum kit in sheets, with tape on the cymbals and pillows underneath. Jonny would be sitting on the bed, Chris would be standing up in one corner, Guy would be sitting in a chair, and I'd be squeezed into this corner just jamming away.

Jonny would sleep in there, too, so he'd have to climb over tape recorders and clothes and all sorts of shit to get into bed."

When it came time to pick a name, Tim Crompton, one of the band's roomies and a musician himself, had a name for a band, simply called the Coldplay. Tim tired of the name and "gave" it to the guys, giving them permission to run with it. "Tim had a band that used to go through six names every week, and the Coldplay was one of the ones they came up with, so we just took it," says Champion. The Coldplay, taken from a little-known book of poetry, *Child's Reflections, Coldplay,* was born with Chris Martin on lead vocals, piano, and rhythm guitar, Jonny Buckland on lead guitar, Guy Berryman on bass, and Wil Champion behind the drums.

The Guys: "I Saw Sparks"
Each of the members of Coldplay was raised in a comfortable, solid, middle-class family with a strong background in religion and a tight family bond. No broken marriages or broken homes here, no dysfunctional families, no drug-addicted siblings, no "wrong side of the tracks" or "chip on the shoulder" to speak of. This is not the type of band that wrecks hotel rooms or turns their backstage area into a battle zone. And sorry, no band member is from Aberdeen and no band member claimed to have lived under a bridge. School, sports, music, religion, and family. Nothing drastic and certainly nothing too melodramatic. Living proof that you, too, can have a normal and stable childhood and still go on to be the world's biggest pop star. Martin defends the band's upbringings in a July 2000 *NME* article. "It's far more rock 'n' roll for us to just be honest

and, you know, we haven't had a particularly rock 'n' roll upbringing. It's hard to validate why we're here, and I hate that." "Apparently Joe Strummer was a middle-class boy. It's much better to be honest about it," says Champion. "There is nothing worse than people pretending to be something they aren't. You've got to be true to what you are." In a interview with KNRK-FM in Portland, Oregon (which was the very first commercial radio station in America to play Coldplay), Martin even went so far as to say, "We don't see ourselves as cool guys in a cool band. We do things that simply aren't cool . . . like wearing white socks with black shoes." Oftentimes, the band and especially Martin had to actually defend their turf while speaking to *Melody Maker* in July 2000. "Of course there's a nasty side to us. But you don't show things like that in interviews. We find it much easier to be nicer. To be civil. Wil is the nicest bloke in the world, but if you take his seat on the bus, then you've had it. There's a nasty side to everyone . . . even dustmen."

Chris Martin—
"You Don't Know How Lovely You Are"
Truly the front man. Truly the spokesperson and, of course, the "heart and soul" of Coldplay. He's the star, the centerpiece that every great band needs to have. He's the lead singer, front and center, who guys envy and women adore. Though Coldplay would not exist if one of the four departed, Coldplay would not even be a DNA cell without Martin and the role he plays as public leader. Not surprisingly, he is the trickiest one to figure out. While being the most outgoing and most gracious of the four, he is also the most difficult one to get a handle on.

Martin claims that he maintains three constants in his life: 1) a turbulent relationship with women that continues to drive his song writing; 2) a fear of dying prematurely; and 3) a preoccupation with hair loss. He is quick to say to anyone associated with Coldplay and within shouting distance "thank you," or rather, "thanks a lot for all that you've done and all that you're doing for us." This would include anyone from their manager, a record label representative, a radio DJ, or even the roadie in charge of Scotch taping the set list on Martin's vocal monitor. It's sincere and humble as all hell, and it makes even the lowest crew member on the Coldplay totem pole want to kill for the band. As early as 2000, *NME* called Martin, "A subject ripe for investigation.. Martin doesn't drink, smoke, or take drugs. He's pretty unusual. He has a Christian-like zeal about him, as if he's enamored by life and its myriad opportunities." It was backstage at RFK Stadium in Washington, D.C. in May of 2001 where I got my first taste of Martin's humble pie and that Christian-like zeal.

I'm really stressed. I worry because my hair is falling out and I don't know if that's important. Will people still buy our records if we all lose our hair? [Chris Martin]

Coldplay had just finished their set on the main stage of the enormous HFStival, an annual festival put on by WHFS-FM in Washington, D.C. According to Coldplay it was a brutal show, similar to the experiences the band had been having on the radio festival circuit that they were currently part of, including WBCN's River Rave in Boston and KROQ's Weenie Roast in Los Angeles. The annual HFStival was the granddaddy of them all; a sold-out, daylong festival that crams over 65,000 people into D.C.'s enormous RFK football stadium.

Coldplay was the third band on an eight-band bill that included Limp Bizkit, Godsmack, and the Deftones, the only British act on this testosterone-fueled rock fest, and, yes . . . they were out of place. Sorry to say, I was the one responsible for booking them, but this is standard fare when you are trying like mad to break a band in America. You need airplay and you need radio station support. One way, and sometimes the only way, to go about this is to get your band into these festivals. This part of the "business" secures airplay and puts your band in front of thousands of people—in this case, over 65,000 of them. Granted, all 65,000 came to "rock" and along comes this midtempo act from across the Atlantic playing their sensitive brand of pop. Challenging to say the least, if not incredibly humbling for any band of Coldplay's nature. Well, maybe the band would disagree but, Coldplay's set was a heart-wrenching, leave-it-all-on-the-stage performance that included Martin bringing a sweat-soaked girl from the enormous mosh pit onstage to accompany the band. Sitting the girl right next to him, they shifted into a breathtaking performance of "Trouble." Quite the gamble to include this piano-laced ballad on a setlist for music fans clamoring for metal jams, but it became one of the highlights of the day and cemented Coldplay into HFStival and Washington, D.C. folklore. Remembers APD Bob Waugh of the radio station WHFS. "We were really gun shy about putting Coldplay on the same bill as some of those harder bands. But when Chris Martin brought up that girl during 'Trouble,' it cleared any doubt we would have about them. I remember watching the girl as she sat next to him on the piano bench; she was just crying and mouthing the words to the song. A true moment to witness."

It was after that set that I became truly "Martinized." Just minutes after their set, Chris asked me to walk with him to get something to eat in the VIP tent backstage. I remember promoters of the concert, stagehands, radio station employees, and other record label executives in the VIP tent watching me in awe and envy as the two of us casually strolled the area in search of leftover hospitality food. This again was and remains to be the every-man quality that Martin possess. "What can we do, what can I do, to make your job easier, Gary? Remember, we are all on the same team," he said as we sat down with a plate of cold deli meats. These are words of gold that any music executive who works with any artist on any level would die to hear; words that put us on the same level. Here's a guy who just won over an angry rock mob of 65,000 with his brand of unconventional modern music, turning to me and asking what he can do to help out with *my* job. Right then, I knew Chris Martin avoided as much as possible being put on a pedestal. He craved to be equals with everyone, especially with one who was part of his team.

The band's identity is a direct reflection of Martin's dualistic personality, confident but self-doubting, assured but self-destructive. Certain but angst-ridden while being friendly, yet moody as fuck. You can glean this not simply by spending a day with him; you can get all this in one *conversation* with the guy. Martin is an emotional melting pot. He stresses and overanalyzes women, hair loss, mortality, and, especially in the bands' early stages, is fraught with conflict between his Christian beliefs and life as a pop icon in a rock 'n' roll band. "You never know what Chris Martin you'll get. His answers will change with his moods, but one thing's for sure—what you will get from Chris will be honest and real," says manager Holmes.

Martin was raised in Devon, England, by an accountant father and biology teacher mother. He is the eldest of five kids, and typical of many firstborns, he is a self-proclaimed worrier and a proud overachiever. Claiming to have had a "pretty idyllic" childhood, Martin enjoyed a solid family life in the countryside. "I grew up listening to cheesy stuff, and it wasn't until I roomed with Jonny and our friend Tim that I discovered things like early R.E.M., the Cure, and Echo and the Bunnymen. I didn't have a clue about anything that went on outside of my own town. Until I went to London, I didn't really know anything." During a radio interview, at WLIR Long Island, he told the DJ, "Devon is kinda hicksville. We just listened to local tractor adverts. There wasn't a lot of music around. I got a tape of music for free with a box of breakfast cereal. That was the only music I had for a year until Michael Jackson's *Bad* came out and we all got into that. My dad listened to a lot of cool country music like Johnny Cash and Hank Williams." It

We're confident in our ability, but surprised when anyone thinks we're that good. That is what categorizes our thinking. [Jonny Buckland]

Buckland was raised in the peculiar, small, and Celtic North Wales town of Mold. Mold happens to be the birthplace of Karl Wallanger of the Waterboys and World Party fame, and eighties U2 wannabes the Alarm. Raised by a science teacher dad and music teacher mom, Buckland started playing guitar by age eleven. He grew up listening to his dad's record collection that included the Beatles, Jimi Hendrix, and Eric Clapton. "That's about when I first started playing my older brother's guitar. One of the first things I was trying to work out by myself was the Happy Mondays' 'Kinky Afro.' " By age fifteen, there wasn't a day that would go by where Jonny wasn't playing along with such powerhouses as My Bloody Valentine. "The Stone Roses and Happy Mondays were just a lot cooler than anything I'd ever heard before. It just seemed like they were having a good time making great songs," Buckland told *Guitar Player* magazine. As time went on, his guitar playing matured, as did his taste in rock music. "The band that really got me into wanting to be in a band was U2 with their *Rattle and Hum* record," he remembers.

Buckland would be a vintage Academy Award nominee for Best Supporting Actor. He prefers the background not only socially, but on stage, as well. He'd rather let his guitar work, the signature hum-along chiming riffs that have become such a major part of Coldplay's signature sound, do the talking for him. Though over time as you get to know him, he makes you feel like you have a new best friend, he is not a guy that would approach a stranger or

even someone that he's met before, but he's open and accommodating if that person approaches him. Though all four are students of pop music history, it is Buckland and Berryman who were the most open to talk about and explore new music discoveries. On the bus touring with the band in the Midwest in the winter of 2003, while everyone else went to their bunks, it was Buckland and Berryman who stayed up to the morning hours with me drinking wine and talking about their newfound love for the Beatles' *White Album*. Still in their early twenties, they were able to listen to Beatles records and find different ways to worship the Fab Four. "Listen to that bass line . . . man, pure genius," Buckland said while "Dear Prudence" was playing on the tour bus stereo. He continues on like only a true Beatlehead would, "Do you hear what McCartney is doing? It's so easy to listen to the harmony of a Beatle song . . . that's what we are trained to hear first. But what could get lost sometimes is how fucking amazing they were as musicians. They were blazing new roads that they probably didn't even know they were making . . . amazing."

Important note: the word "amazing" is, by far and without debate, Buckland's favorite word in the entire English language. Like the other three, Buckland's a combination of youthful innocence and old soul. And like the others, he, too, is genuinely interested in not only what you do for the band, but who you are as a person and what you have to say.

Wil Champion—
"Give Me Real, Don't Give Me Fake"

An appropriate namesake for the member in the band who possesses, well . . . the strongest will, Wil is also the most intense and the one who is most concerned and connected with the band's integrity and credibility. Wil told *NME* that his most important contribution to the band is, "Saying no. I like saying no. Often I have to say, 'No, we're not doing that.' " He is the benchmark and if he likes a song that Martin brings to the band, then chances are the song will get recorded. You would be hard pressed to find another drummer who has more say in a band's overall presentation. "Everything the band does has to pass the 'Wil test' . . . everything," says Holmes. "Wil's the one I have to impress," smiles Martin. "If he goes 'urgh,' then I have to acknowledge it's no good.

It's become one of my great hobbies in life . . . trying to convince Wil that my songs are any good." Even Martin's lyrics must pass the test. Martin explains during an aftershow party in Minneapolis, "The original first phrase of 'Politix' was 'Look at earth from outer space. Isn't this a crazy place.' " He continues, "Wil quickly glared at me and gave me that look. He thought the line to be cheesy, too trite, and now looking back—it was. Needless to say I changed that line in the song." Wil was also the member of the group that most opposed ABC-TV using the song "Yellow" for the network's all-important winter 2000–2001 TV campaign. "We were young and quite honestly didn't even know what ABC-TV was or what they were planning to do with the song," remembers Martin. "Well, once we found out, it was Wil who yelled the loudest. That would be the first and last time we would let that happen." Champion remembers the unpleasant moment as well. "If it had been a hundred percent up to us, we would have said no. It was out of our control, I guess. When it's being used to sell someone else's product, then I don't think it's a good idea at all." He went on to tell the *Chicago Sun Times*, "If it's used for trailing programs, I don't mind that. But we'd never, ever advertise Coke or something like that. Especially traveling as much as we do, I just get so sick of adverts. You can't escape consumerism on American TV." Though "Yellow" was eventually approved for use, Wil's objection led to the current ban on all Coldplay advertising endorsements. Coldplay has since turned down well over four million dollars' worth of offers that could have easily set the band up for life. The "Wil test" has many obstacles.

Champion was born and raised in Southampton by his co-archeologist parents. Wil's dad, as Martin puts it, "is the Michael Jackson of British archeology."

Champion is also the bands official "jock." He is rarely seen backstage without a basketball in his hands. Coldplay now has it written in their performance contracts for concert promoters that a basketball hoop be part of their tour rider. During breaks from soundchecks and interviews, Champion can be found shooting hoops backstage and looking for opponents to take him on in a game of "horse." He's an avid supporter of his hometown soccer team, Southampton F.C., but it is the American NBA that has become his number one sport. As Coldplay began reaching new heights of fame and popularity, Champion has struck up close friendships with the NBA elite, including Dallas Maverick all-stars Steve Nash and Dirk Nowinski.

He did not go down your typical drummers' path of "once a drummer always a drummer." Unlike his drumming peers, he is not obsessed with the drummers' drummer guys such as John Bonham or Stewart Copeland. Champion plays a wide range of instruments and actually went to the University College in London wanting to play guitar. "As a musician, he's got the most amazing sense of melody. He can play just about anything," says Martin. As a matter of fact, Wil can be heard playing acoustic guitar on many songs during the band's early days of doing acoustic sets for radio stations and record store appearances.

While all four members are mature beyond their years, it is Wil who takes more of a fatherly role in the group. The other three look to Wil for reassurance and confirmation on ideas, concepts, and thoughts they may have for the band.

When asked about this book and how he wanted to be portrayed, Champion paused for a beat and looked me square in the eye and warmly said, "Just write the truth, and please get the truth right."

We're just lucky, I think. I'd like to say that we're great and we make great records, but people who are really great most of the time don't sell records and people that are really shit sell loads of 'em. [Wil Champion]

With the help of their college mate and now official manager Phil Harvey, Coldplay raised £1,500 to cut a record. This three-song recording, called *Safety*, included "Bigger, Stronger," "Such a Rush," and "No More Keeping My Feet on the Ground." Released in May of '98, the EP intended for friends, family, and a small list of record company executives is now out of print with no plans for reissue. It now will occasionally pop up on eBay, going for as much as $500 a copy! It was the latter of the three songs that woke up Dan Keeling's ear; Keeling knew the band needed work, but was impressed enough to know they could go somewhere. A relationship between Keeling and Coldplay was born. "It just overwhelmed me. I wanted to stay cool, but I could only hold off calling until Saturday morning," recalls Keeling. Guy Berryman explains, "Dan is our record label guy and our best friend all in one. After Phil Harvey, Dan is Coldplay's sixth member." "We go at it at times with Dan—Chris and Dan especially knocked heads during the recording of *Parachutes*— but it's out of respect and friendship that he is able to do what he does," adds Buckland.

I think of us as the people who've been let into the party who shouldn't really be there. [Chris Martin]

Over the next year, Coldplay played the juggling game of being full-time university students and part-time musicians. The reversal started taking place in the spring of 1999. In April of that year, Coldplay released a three-song CD single on the very hip and credible English label Fierce Panda, with the A-side of "Brothers and Sisters," backed by B-sides "Easy to Please" and "Only Superstition." Up until recently the only way to obtain a copy

of this was via import eBay. A small independent label, Brash Music, out of Atlanta, acquired North American distribution rights from Fierce Panda and re-released the three-song collection as the *Brothers and Sisters* EP with the original artwork and song order. "We planned to only release five thousand copies, but by street date of the EP [11/18/03] the orders more than tripled. Retail knows there is a large and growing legion of Coldplay fans who will want this in their collection," said Brash Music employee Shawn Moseley.

Only 2,000 copies were originally pressed, but it caught the attention of *NME* and a long love/hate relationship with *NME* officially kicked off. "There are a lot of people who work at *NME* who are on our side and like us," Martin explains, "but there is a certain camp at that place that think we are the devils and will do anything to smash us down." *NME* reviewed the CD single and called Coldplay "a band to watch for 2000." More important than the review was that the CD single also caught the attention of Radio One DJ Steve Lamacq. Lamacq featured "Brothers and Sisters" on his Evening Sessions show, helping the single reach a rather humble but impressive number 92 on the British national singles chart. "Steve Lamacq is a guy we always looked up to. We love his taste in music and he was the first bloke to put us on the radio. We like him because he took a chance on us, but it was his musical taste that cemented our friendship," says Berryman fondly. Buckland adds, "He gave us our first break. We did the Evening Session show before we were signed or anything. We played three songs on the air, 'Brothers and Sisters' and a new song at the time called 'Shiver.' 'Shiver' was done in this horrible three-four time . . . we were so nervous—

but that was the very first time we played that song live." This shot from Lamacq and Radio One served as a critical springboard to garner major label attention and a small but intense bidding war.

In the summer of 1999, the bidding war came to a head and Coldplay went with EMI/Parlaphone, home to legendary and substantial acts such as the Beatles, Pink Floyd, Blur, and band favorite Radiohead. It was Dan Keeling, who had passed on the group only a year earlier, who signed the band. The group solidified their recording contract by signing their deal in the heart of London's Leicester Square and then followed that with agreeing to a publishing deal with BMG Music Publishing that took place on the lake in Hyde Park. The guys had an executive of BMG row them to the center of the park's lake for the ceremony of signing. 1999 was also the year that the guys (minus Guy) earned their degrees from UCL; Chris in ancient world studies, Jonny in astronomy, and Wil in anthropology. July was the month set for the band to hit the studio with Ken Nelson in the producer's chair. It proved to be a match made in the musical heavens as Nelson has held permanent residence as the producer for all of Coldplay's studio recordings. He even joined the band onstage at the 2004 Grammy Awards where Champion grabbed the microphone and proclaimed to the billions watching the awards show that Nelson is "the most fabulous record producer in the world." "Ken quickly became our coproducer. If I or anyone else has an idea and he doesn't think it's very good, we don't do it, and vice versa. Ken is the master of making sure we keep the emotion of the song intact and that we don't ruin that," says Martin. "Ken is not your typical record producer with a big ego. He's into

capturing the mood of a band and not so obsessed with getting the process right," says drummer Champion. Adds Buckland, "Ken operated like a band member. He helped us trim the fat and told us when a performance was cool or when it was complete rubbish. We needed that."

Coldplay also earned a spot on the coveted new band stage at the 1999 Glastonbury Festival. Remembers drummer Champion, "Glastonbury was brilliant. You grow up hearing about these classic Glastonbury sets. For a British band, it's the pinnacle . . . the coolest gig you can do. We started off on the new band stage, then moved to the side stage in 2000, and then we graduated to the main stage in 2001." Berryman had a different view. "I had never been or even heard of Glastonbury before we played the new band stage. But once we did, we knew we just had to play as headliners one day."

The early signs of genuine uneasiness and apprehension that coincided with the pressures of a major label debut slapped Coldplay in the face and especially smacked Chris Martin hard. Things had truly hit "high speed" and during the early sessions for the debut album, Champion walked out claiming things had become too tense and edgy. "Things were going wrong in the studio and I told Wil it was his fault, telling him he was shit. I was so nervous of us fucking up our chance that I became a fucking twat," remembers Martin. "The first few weeks of recording were stressful. We couldn't seem to get anything done. I think the only thing we were pleased with was a new version of 'Don't Panic,' but everything else went really badly," recalls Buckland. For about a week or so, Coldplay wasn't even a functioning band; Martin had to plead with Champion more than once to return. He eventually caved when a promise was kept that everything with Coldplay be split four ways, 25 percent of everything. The democracy of the band was now formalized and on paper. This split would include songwriting, songwriting credits, performance fees, royalties, etc. Martin didn't hesitate and agreed to all of Champion's demands and the drummer rejoined the group as the *Parachute* sessions continued. "I didn't want all the fucking money. I didn't want any more than the others. Did I really want to spend two weeks in court someday down the line arguing with my closest mates about who wrote what? Not all bands work that way and I've gotten into arguments with some about it. But going through that experience made me realize that our chemistry is special. I can't do it without them—all of them—and vice versa," said Martin.

"I want to live life . . . and I wanna fly, I'll never come down. And live my life and have friends around." —"We Never Change"

The sessions continued to drag on as the band managed to put just three songs down to tape. "See You Soon," the new version of "Don't Panic," and "High Speed." "It was the worst week ever," recalls Martin. "For a week Coldplay didn't exist. Largely it was my fault—well, it *was* my fault—there was a serious lack of communication. To mark the end of this horrible, horrible week, I decided I'd get drunk just to make myself even more miserable. It was Guy—Guy was feeding me vodka and cranberry. All I remember is playing harmonica on the street trying to eat Guy's chips and then trying to sleep in Wil's room 'cause he

wasn't there. Now I just don't drink. I hate it." Martin has not been drunk since. "Chris brings quite enough spice to our lives without alcohol being involved. That was a horrible time and one that I would never go through again," explains Buckland. Keeling remembers, "It [the sessions] didn't have any of their passion, their energy. It was just limp. I drove straight down to the studio and had a very tense meeting. Chris didn't like what we had to say, which was basically, 'do it again.' They're a close unit and they don't like people sticking their noses in."

One day we feel like we are in the greatest band in the world and the next day someone will come up to one of us and say how great we are and all I can think is, Okay. What's the joke? What's the punchline?
[Chris Martin]

Parlaphone, fearing more delays and wanting to bank on the growing buzz that was being generated, decided to use those three songs and throw in "Bigger, Stronger" and "Such a Rush" to make up *The Blue Room* EP. This EP would serve as the official introduction to the general public and was released in November 1999. It proved to be a great ploy as *NME* called the EP, "The ideal debut. Clearly Coldplay has established itself as a band to adore for 2000." Martin, as said in a *L.A. Times* interview a year later, remembers the labors of the early sessions. "There must have been six times where we just sat around and everyone was staring at the floor." He goes on, "It was not gonna get finished . . . this is it . . . we're done with. But we just kept chipping away, and I thought, Well, if we put this much passion into it, someone's got to like it. Something this painful can't be a complete waste of time."

It was Steve Lamacq, now a trusted friend of Radio One, who was the first to play "Yellow"; it was July of 2000. It was Glastonbury Festival time again, and this time Coldplay had graduated to the second stage to play a 1:00 P.M. set in front of ten thousand-plus . . . easily their most prodigious gig to date. At the end of their closing number, "Shiver," Martin laid down the gauntlet with this short but subversive speech. "Thank you for coming out at 1:00 P.M. to see us. Next time we'll be Bon Jovi size and we'll be headlining the main stage." Martin had this to say about the 2000 Glastonbury experience when asked by *NME*: "Glastonbury was just brilliant; probably the happiest weekend I've ever had. My childhood dreams come true; playing in front of loads of people, getting to sit with Jo Wiley on a bale of hay, and getting to see David Gray. It was such a cool experience." He gushed on, "It was by miles the biggest gig we've played and God, we were nervous. We knew it was important for us not to muck it up." Songs like the closer "Shiver" and "Don't Panic" were standouts, but it was "Yellow" that became the official anthem of Glastonbury 2000. The boys knew the performance of "Yellow"

had to be a defining moment for them. "We really wanted to play 'Yellow' well . . . with a bit of soul, 'cause we knew that there'd be a lot of attention on it. The last couple of times we played it were absolutely rubbish," said Martin. They played between Toplander and David Gray, causing *Melody Maker* to gush, "They were the highlight of Glastonbury. Lay to rest any doubts, Coldplay, with Chris Martin in front, is a music leader." The show and the reviews that flowed in were the match that lit the cannon's fuse for "Yellow." Berryman remembers the show fondly by saying, "It was amazing to play in front of that many people on such a nice day. I was really nervous for about the first three songs, but then I started feeling really comfortable. We nailed 'Yellow.' "

"Oh yeah, your skin and bones, turn into something beautiful." —"Yellow"

"Yellow" was released June 26, just days after the mouth-dropping Glastonbury gig. The song screamed on to the charts, debuting at number 4 and going right to number 1 the next week. The song was picked up not only by Radio One, but added to the highly competitive XFM and Virgin Radio playlists, as well. Jonny Buckland remembers the moment he heard the news of "Yellow" going number 1. "It was nothing but great. I was on holiday in the South of France and Phil Harvey tracked me down. I was in a swimming pool and I thought, Well, this is Duran Duran shit happening here. It was amazing."

"Shock . . . horror!" Berryman chimes in "We weren't really expecting to do anything like that. We thought, if we were lucky, we might scrape the

Top Twenty; but this was way beyond our wildest dreams." While the recording of the album was tense, stressful, and at times unbearable, Champion remembers the recording of "Yellow" quite differently. " 'Yellow' will always be a happy song because it represents a happy time for us. A lot of time in the studio was spent arguing and fighting. But that day was a really good day." Martin concurs, "It was amazing for us when it went number 1, because we could remember every single note, where it was written, where the artwork was done, and every nuance about the song. It made it all worthwhile." Always the humble one, when "Yellow" went to number 1, Martin said to *NME* that, "Funny enough, I woke up this morning thinking, Wouldn't it be nice to be number 2, because so many great records have been number two: 'Strawberry Fields,' 'Bittersweet Symphony,' 'Paranoid Android,' classics."

Inspired by a sun-drenched Welsh countryside, Martin penned the lyrics to the song with ease, and it became Coldplay's flag to wave. "I was just fiddling around on the guitar one day and it came to me. It was quick. At first I was singing it like a Neil Young song, and that melody came out and it sounded wicked. The first verse and the chorus came really quickly to me, and I thought it was beautiful. That was the very first time I felt that way, 'cause usually I doubt all my songs in the beginning." Martin explained the song during an interview with Seattle radio station KNDD. "The song is about devotion. About doing something for someone and being pleased about it." Many in the Coldplay camp, including Martin, felt that the reason why "Yellow" took off was because it was "romantic and uncynical"; a far cry from what radio was playing during the summer of 2000. If radio wasn't enough to make "Yellow" a staple in England, then the video sure pushed the song over the top. The video was simplistic beauty, capturing both the vibe of the song and stunning emotion of Martin's vocal delivery. Shot with a single camera on a typically cold and dreary English afternoon, the video nails the chiming, bittersweet beauty conveyed by the song. Martin explains the behind-the-scenes luck of how the video came together.

"I had to do it alone for various reasons. The guys all had personal business to tend to so I was left alone. The weather was just so bad; you know, it rains a lot in Britain. We had one day to shoot 'cause we were going on tour the next day—we, I, had no choice. It was meant to be a sunny video on the beach, but we had to change that. There were all these extras waiting to be part of the video shoot, but they were all miserable and all they wanted to do was to go home. So I just walked along the beach and sang to the camera. The whole thing took twenty minutes and we all went home."

We wake up thinking we are the best band in the world. I'm playing with my three best friends and making better music than anyone right now.

[Chris Martin]

July 10, 2000 was the UK release date of their now highly anticipated debut, *Parachutes*. Produced by Ken Nelson, the recording not only took place in Liverpool's Par Studios as well as Matrix, Wessex, and Rockfield Studios in London. The band could not have been more relieved about the completion of the sessions. "The day we were happy was the day we stopped working on the bloody thing," Martin told *Melody Maker*. "We don't think of the album in terms of forty-two minutes of music. We think in terms of nine weeks of argument and pain. We were so tense for ages. We put so much into our recordings. We got as much passion in as possible, especially in songs like 'Yellow.' " While the nine weeks proved difficult and painstaking for the band, a recording style was used that all four members were insistent upon; it was this basic, old-school recording process that practically saved the album and, in turn, the band. Buckland shared his thoughts with *Guitar Player*. "We wanted to capture the unpretentious vibe of old Motown tracks while maintaining a big, modern rock sound. When you listen to those records, they have such an immediacy and personality to them. We wanted our tracks to have that same spark, and we decided the best way to do that was to record live." In ways that the Beatles would have been proud (for the well-publicized fact that they would do up to seventy takes of a song during their later years), songs such as the opener "Don't Panic" were recorded over and over because simple overdubs killed the

overall feel of the song. Explains Buckland, "On that song, it just felt right to play these glowing, delay-laden interjections with the lyrics in the chorus. I don't think I would have come up with that part if I was busy overdubbing guitars. Right then, live, I was reacting to the band and the song. We were looking for a raw, rich sound that's not too slick. That's what is quite unpleasant about a lot of pop records. It's just so perfect that you can't imagine people onstage singing those things live." It was that innocent band magic that kept their heads up. "It was like, 'Yeah, all right, we get it.' This is why we're here. Playing live and all of us agreeing that the songs must be done live in the studio, saved us," claimed Martin.

The naïveté of going into the recording studio to make an entire record almost caused the band to implode. "We thought we could do it in two weeks, man. You know, like The Band or something. Well, after two weeks, we hadn't done anything. We kept setting deadlines and never making them. It was pretty manic and painful, but in the end it was all worth it," says Martin.

The album was dubbed *Parachutes* because, as Martin explains it, "Parachutes get you out of bad situations. The album was going to be called *Don't Panic*, but *Parachutes* seemed to fit. Some of our songs have a bleak outlook, you know, and then the parachute is pulled and you can enjoy it. But really, the album's called *Parachutes* cause we had to decide a title. But it does work. Often the things that fit best are the things that have to be decided very quickly. Like racing out of the house and choosing the first thing that looks good to wear is usually the best thing to wear for that moment."

Champion backs up the decision for the title. "A lot of the album has to do with everyday problems. It doesn't really matter who you are. It's not necessarily about us. They are mostly about being in the middle of everything and trying to get away from it. Everyone can use a parachute from time to time."

The album rocketed right to the top, debuting at number 1 in the UK with more than 70,000 copies sold in its first week, and proceeded to stay in the Top 10 for over thirty-three weeks. The album went on to sell over 300,000 in the UK alone; just a tad over the estimated figure of 40,000 by its label, Parlaphone! Coldplay, on just their first record, secured a permanent position in Britain's music elite by writing uncompromising, beautiful, simple songs that gently pulled at the heartstrings of an entire nation. Somewhere in between the confident but vulnerable guitar playing of Jonny Buckland, the melodic baselines of Guy Berryman, thoughtful and precise drumming of Wil Champion, and lead man Chris Martin's stark, tenor vocals seemed to be answers for the heart and soul of their home country. What helped Coldplay stand head and shoulders above their steep competition was their sincere optimism. The songs seemed to start with sadness, but by song's end find their own parachute and land in a better place where truth and honesty win out. "We just want the songs to reflect reality," says Martin. That quote was found and said more than once and seemed to be a battle cry for the band. Martin continues, "A lot of the album is dark, and a lot of it is light. It's a bit of both, hopefully ending on an optimistic note. I've always been taught that things could be shit, but you've got to tackle them with guts. Otherwise you're just going to give up."

NME gave it a "nine out of ten" and it was the magazine's lead review in its week of release. This album was a rare beast. It proved to be a record that simply transcended; it had no boundaries. *Parachutes* seemed to unite students, young adults, tastemakers, hipsters, ravers, and yuppies alike. The album saw no segregation between style, class, race, color, or sex. *Melody Maker* called it "an original breed, a stunning debut and true accomplishment." *Q* magazine called the debut, "Love letters of hurt, faith, and redemption. Coldplay deserves their number one debut!" Martin put the newfound success into his own warped perspective. "People have got into this album, and that's wicked. But dealing with fame is another matter. Your first album goes number one, and all it means is more promo, more pressure, and more time spent away from home."

Of course, with all the wonderful praise and admiration came a certain backlash. Get on top and someone will inevitably try to bring you down. The first wave of negativity came from none other than one of the founding fathers of Brit pop himself, Mr. Alan McGee. McGee, Creation Records founder and, among many things, Jesus and Mary Chain and Oasis svengali said, "Coldplay make bed wetters' music. They are bed wetters and opportunists who care more about passing their class exams." The members of Coldplay handled this and all of their foes with their now standard demeanor of class and dignity. Coldplay refused to get into a pissing match, exactly what the hungry beast, known as the English tabloids, loves to feast on. A classic Blur–Oasis dogfight, this was not to be; Coldplay would not step down to McGee's turf. They would not lower themselves to his level, despite the tabloid's wishes for them to do so. When finally pressed against the ropes, Martin would only defend his band. He said this to *Flaunt* magazine, "We don't give a shit what people think. We do what we want. Punk is doing what you want. It's not about wearing leather and flashy shades and acting like every other rock star."

We are successful because we're fucking good, we work damned hard, and just maybe because we're jammy bastards. [Chris Martin]

In *Pulse* magazine his response was, "It doesn't really affect what you think, it does drive you on. It's like *Rocky IV* or something. You've got to have your enemy to focus on and then it makes you train hard and work hard and eventually win the boxing match." Finally, in *Q* magazine a couple of years later, Martin opened up a bit more. "I would like to shake Alan McGee by the hand. Quite right of him to give us a kick up the arse. I say, 'Bring it on, because it makes me think, I'll show you.' He's trying to hurt me so I go away and train like a monkey and do incredible press-ups and listen to loads of music and write songs better than the Hives. Then I'll say to Alan McGee, 'Thanks a lot, man.' "

The branding of choirboys and posh, upper-middle-class tarts was already in the works, but the music was speaking loudly for the group; even some outspoken leaders in "the land of cool" were siding with Coldplay. Liam Gallagher of Oasis took an immediate liking to the band, saying, "They're cool, man. I believe him when he sings. He means it. A lot of bands don't mean it. I don't know, but I believe him.." Liam literally grabbed the band backstage after a gig at London's Sheperds Bush Empire in late 2000 to tell them that the song "Yellow" was the sole reason why he was able to start writing new songs again. Remembers Martin, "The Gallaghers said to me, 'Don't worry 'bout fookin' McGee. We like ya.' " Credibility would also quickly come to their rescue in the form of Simon Williams, cofounder of Fierce Panda. "Radiohead and Jeff Buckley inspire great loyalty. . . . Coldplay should and will be counted among those artists." And, of course, the bands members' upbringing and university-educated background didn't do much to trim the critics. "I'm not going to be like, 'Hi, Mom, hi, Dad. I'm going off to do some coke, can you make sure my trousers are ironed?' " "We aren't that nice," adds Buckland, "but it pisses me off that it's such a terrible thing to be. We can be arseholes, but most of the time we're all right. On balance, I'd take nice over being called a cunt any day."

You couldn't look at any review in any magazine without all the references and comparisons: "A mild Jeff Buckley." "Radiohead lite." "This year's Travis." Martin defends these comparisons and brushes them off by saying, "Those comparisons are always being made. It's not something that pisses us off, because we love those artists. But we all are inspired by different kinds of stuff like Neil Young, the Flaming Lips, and Dylan." He goes on with a smile to say, "If you're a middle-class white boy singing in a vaguely high-pitched voice, you're going to be compared to Radiohead and Dave Matthews. But it's better than being compared to 'N Sync. We know we can't dance and we don't look like 'N Sync, but when we sing about something, we really mean it." Coldplay is always one to wear their influences on their sleeves and quite frankly, they are not ashamed to admit them to anyone who asks. Explains Martin, "I love the fact the word 'influence' is just another word for 'stealing something from someone.' Another word for copying. We, as a band, have loads of, umm . . . influences."

After the American press, like clockwork, came the celebrities. Already having called Radiohead their own, the entertainment industry's fashionably elite was quick to pick up on the next one. Chris, Jonny, Guy, and Wil, who hadn't even set foot on American soil, were already Hollywood's toast of the town.

Kirsten Dunst: "I love Coldplay and their hit 'Yellow.' I love his voice, and their whole CD is great to listen to. Every single song is a great song. Chris Martin has such a cute little accent when he sings."

Renée Zellweger: "Right now I'm listening to this band from England. Coldplay. . . . Ohhhh, you have to get it. They are so good."

Justin Timberlake: "Whoever writes their melodies, like that song 'Yellow,' that's an incredible melody. That's so Beatles. It's ridiculous."

Kylie Minogue: "Coldplay was like a beautiful secret, and then I told everyone about it."

Rob Thomas (Matchbox 20): " 'Yellow' came on the radio, and for the first time in four or five years, I drove around the block so I could hear it. Chris Martin's voice has a quality all its own, and there's a yearning to it."

It wouldn't be long as to when the virtual list of who's who in Hollywood would be calling to inquire when Coldplay was coming to the States. Publicists from New York to Los Angeles were now calling Coldplay's label, their management, and booking agent inquiring about the band. "Our office started getting calls from all these actors' publicists and their personal assistants asking when Coldplay is coming to play and how my client needs . . . has . . . to get in," said manager Holmes.

Next up was the "golden ticket." The elusive all-access pass to fame and fortune in America. The quickest, the trickiest, but at the same time the easiest way to meet your destiny in the States; the one medium that *any* band that wants, needs, desires, and prays for music stardom— R-A-D-I-O. American radio and all its splendor. Yes, your dreams can come true if you are able to get your music somehow played in this five-star club. And yes, your dreams can be squashed, evaporated, washed away, and destroyed by *not* getting airplay. A simple fact is that nine out of ten bands released in America in any given year fail. A whopping .5 percent (yes, that is less than 1 percent) of all records released in that year achieve "platinum" status. That's record sales over one million, and that is still less than 1 percent of the population of the United States! The unequaled and most obvious way to achieve a platinum record is by getting airplay . . . loads, bucketloads, and even more loads of it. A research study in the year 2000 showed that over 80 percent of *all* records bought by the American public were purchased because that person "heard it on the radio." Another 10 percent is from "word of mouth"; what this means is that someone told someone about a record that they heard . . . more than likely on the radio! So safe to say, close to 90 percent, or nine out of ten people in America, will buy a record because they happen to hear the band's current "single" being played on their local radio station.

Coldplay was aware of this and knew the uphill battle and improbable odds they would be facing when they finally come across the Atlantic. "It means a lot to us to get our music heard in America," said Martin. "But at the same time, we don't have any expectations. If we don't make it in America, it won't kill us. We wouldn't be the first band to fail. Now that we are coming over, at the very least, we get a chance to see America." He told *HITS* magazine in late 2000 that, "We're all a bit scared of America, because it's so enormous, and we only see things like Shania Twain. But most of our favorite music is from America. We know there must be something great about it or it wouldn't be able to produce people like Bob Dylan or the Flaming Lips. When all you see is Limp Bizkit, you get sort of a skewed image, but we're quite excited about coming." In an interview with *Pulse* magazine around the same time, Martin said, "If we break, we break. If we don't, it's not going to make us commit suicide. There are a lot of great American bands that aren't big in America."

The blanket that would comfort Coldplay's arrival on American shores, and keep them warm, was radio itself. Depending on whose story you believe, it was KCRW-FM, an NPR station located near the Santa Monica beaches in southern California, that popped Coldplay's cherry on U.S. radio. Nic Harcourt, host of the popular and influential Morning Becomes Eclectic daily morning show, was the very first DJ in the States to take hold of the band. Nic's show, located on the Santa Monica City College campus, is listened to by a cornucopia of southern California's population. College students, yuppies, young adults, film and music industry executives, advertising agencies, hipsters, actors,

and anyone else who craves cutting-edge music listen avidly to KCRW every Monday through Friday from 9:00 A.M. to noon. Harcourt fondly remembers the first time he heard the words "cold" and "play" together. "Dougie and Fran of Travis were in my studio to play guest DJ on my show in July 2000. Dougie said, 'You gotta play this, man,' and excitedly pulled a CD out of his back pocket. But the CD was cracked. It was his own copy of *Parachutes* and both he and Fran went on and on about it. Well, we couldn't play it that day, but it took forty-eight hard-searching hours to get hold of an import." He continues, "Upon first listen, I knew this was something deep; Travis was right. Coldplay and Travis share something that is in both their hearts; a respect for song craft . . . for songwriting."

I can't listen to our records. All I hear is the mistakes we made in the songs. [Chris Martin]

KCRW began playing multiple songs from *Parachutes*. Along with "Yellow," KCRW's full time rotation included "Shiver," "Trouble," and "Don't Panic." "It quickly became the in-house favorite with all our DJs at the station. To this day, we take great pride in what we helped start with Coldplay," states Harcourt.

From there the race was on; it was just a matter of time until a big and almighty commercial rock radio station in a major U.S. city grabbed hold of Coldplay. And, of all places, it was in the northwest city of Portland, Oregon. Program director of KNRK-FM Mark Hamilton is a born-and-bred Brit from just outside London. Hamilton, like a smart program director of an alternative rock station should, keeps close ties with his peers back home in the UK. "It was a friend outside of the music business back home who turned me on to it. He kept ranting on about this band called Coldplay. Less than a week after that, I noticed Coldplay entered the UK charts at number one and I tracked down a copy of 'Yellow.' I didn't know, or didn't care for that matter, if they had a label deal in the States or not . . . I was putting this band on my station. I remember playing this import for friends at a party, way before anyone heard of them here, and they all just flipped. I knew I was holding on to something special."

"I put 'Yellow' on the station and my first batch of call-out research.* They "call-out" a seven-to-ten-second hook of a song and ask the person on the other end of the phone to rate the song. After all the votes are tallied, all songs tested are put in a chart-ranking order. Radio station program directors take this information very seriously when determining what song will stay on the airwaves and what song will go. So 'Yellow' came back . . . and wouldn't you know, it came back at number one. Fucking number one! That rarely, if never, happens with a new band. This validated everything I believed from the get-go on this song and this band."

While KNRK and KCRW were playing "Yellow," believe it or not, the band actually had yet to secure a label deal in North America. "We didn't think we would actually get to America on this album," remembers Champion. "We had a number one, but at the time, I suppose, any American

label wasn't gung-ho to take on a band like us. Everything from Britain just seemed to come out and flop in the States." Coldplay had a worldwide deal with EMI (Parlaphone in the UK), but no one in the EMI North American family seemed to be willing to take the shot on four English lads in their early twenties. Sound familiar? Like almost "forty years ago" familiar? Music historians will be quick to point out that in the early 1960s, every major American label had passed on what was to become the world's greatest rock 'n' roll phenomenon, the Beatles. The Beatles' recording home of over four decades, Capitol Records, even passed on signing the group twice! It was the small but credible Nettwerk Records that came to the rescue; Nettwerk, a label and management company all in one, discovered Coldplay via its joint venture with Capitol Records and EMI. President of Nettwerk, Terry McBride, jumped at the chance to grab Coldplay, appointing GM of the label, Dave Holmes, to oversee the band and comanage the group with Phil Harvey. Remembers Holmes before his first meeting with the band, "The first time we heard the album and 'Yellow,' we knew we could have a smash on our hands. Then I flew out to England to meet them and I was blown away by their charisma, confidence, their wit, and how professional they were . . . especially Chris."

"We took on the group when they were so young and we immediately saw potential way beyond this album," says McBride. Again, the members of Coldplay were extremely hesitant to make a go of it in America and Martin was quick to tell Holmes about what he believed was a "certain degree of antipathy" with the American rock music fan, but nevertheless, the band signed on with

---

*Call-out research is what radio stations use to monitor how a song on their station "tests."

Nettwerk/Capitol Records and agreed to make—or at least try to make—the United States a part of their impending world supremacy.

It was around this time, as things were beginning to bubble with Nettwerk/Capitol, that the powerful and all-influential juggernaut radio station KROQ-FM in Los Angeles started sniffing around the Coldplay camp. The self-proclaimed "World Famous 106.7, K-ROCK" in Los Angeles is responsible for so many careers of alternative rock stars that even the station itself has lost track of the number. There is not a rock station in America, let alone the western hemisphere, that doesn't look to the mighty call letters on a weekly basis to see what they have just added to their current playlist, what they are playing, and, sadly enough, what they are not playing. While KCRW and KNRK had yet to actually "report" their Coldplay airplay to any trade magazine or public forum (because they were both playing it as an "import" and, as stated, Coldplay had yet to finalize a North American label deal), it was KROQ-Los Angeles that was the very first station to "add" a Coldplay song to their highly coveted and nearly impossible to break into playlist. Sandwiched between the likes of Incubus, Green Day, Limp Bizkit, and Metallica, Coldplay plopped itself right

down in the middle of the modern rock mix. KROQ put "Yellow" on the air on September 1st, 2000 and officially "added" the song September 7th. It was the add "heard around the industry" and KNRK followed; the buzz was on and it was on full force. Nettwerk and Capitol didn't even plan to release the song to radio until January 2001, but the demand for the song was too overwhelming to ignore. Kevin Weatherly, KROQ's highly respected program director, remembers how it went down at KROQ. "Lisa Worden, our music director, brought it in as an import to a music meeting. It was lightning in a bottle for us. We knew very little about the band; didn't even know what record label they were on when we added the song. Doesn't matter where they come from or when they come in because songs like 'Yellow' are timeless."

KNRK in Portland reported their unbelievable number 1 research results and KROQ's tests told them the same thing. This news became industry knowledge and soon radio stations all over the country were asking, "What is a coldplay?" and "Where can I get a copy of the CD?" Coldplay and their song "Yellow" were indeed lightning in a bottle and this bottle was about to be uncorked for all of America to adore.

Most celebrities are quite boring. It's a ridiculously insular world. I think most celebrities, myself included, are just ambitious twats.

[Chris Martin (*NME* interview)]

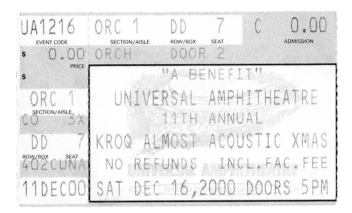

Next up was a meeting with Sylvester Stallone. "We were all excited to meet 'Rocky,' but we also knew he wanted something that we weren't prepared to give him. It was a nice lunch anyway," recalls Berryman. Stallone wanted to use the song "Trouble" for an upcoming movie and the band, being polite and a tad in awe of *Rambo*, waited until they got back to the UK to tell Stallone's people thanks, but no thanks. After a brush with Hollywood royalty, it was off to the KROQ Almost Acoustic Christmas show at the 6,000-plus-seat Universal Amphitheater. The venue is located above the Warner Bros. Studios lot and adjacent to Universal Studios. "If you're gonna do it, you might as well do it in style," said Phil Harvey upon their arrival at the KROQ show. You probably have to go all the way back to February 9, 1964, when the Beatles landed at JFK in New York to play their debut American performance on *The Ed Sullivan Show* to match the leap of faith that a band, any band, from Great Britain had to make to get through their *very* first American concert. Usually there is a thing called a "warm-up gig" that a band

likes to do as a first concert for a new tour, let alone one in America! But leave it to Coldplay to go "trail by fire." Right before the band was to hit the stage for their first ever American performance, Martin's piano went out on him, forcing them to remove "Trouble" from the KROQ set list.

"It was a freak show," remembers Berryman. "They had a revolving stage and we kinda jumped on it and the next thing you know we were in front of six thousand Americans." Buckland chimes in, "We weren't really nervous because we were going from one place to the next in Los Angeles and we didn't have time to really think about it. Probably better that way." The spotlight went down on Chris Martin and Coldplay's first concert was on its way. Like a true veteran, Martin changed the running order of the songs on the spot, after the opener "Don't Panic," saying to the sold-out crowd, "We better play the song you know before you leave your seat to go grab a beer or take a piss." Martin quickly motioned to the boys to jump into "Yellow" and off they went. All of a sudden, Coldplay had won over the sold-out crowd. "I was so nervous for them," remembers Lisa Worden. "I would have been so mad at our audience if they didn't appreciate what we were all witnessing. Their first American show ever, and it was amazing." The review the following Monday in the *Hollywood Reporter* agreed, saying, "Coldplay played the prettiest songs of the night, and the applause from the rock-hungry crowd had to ease the band's nerves."

After meeting the likes of At the Drive-In, Gavin Rosedale, and Gwen Stefani, the band was hustled to an aftershow party at Highway 101 Diner in Hollywood. Just up the block from Capitol Records, it's not exactly the kind of place to have a gathering of any kind, but it was actually the band's idea to host the party there. "We loved the movie, *Swingers*—well, Phil and I did probably more than the others," beams Martin. "When someone asked where we'd like to go, we just said, 'Take us to that diner in that movie *Swingers*.' " Stars like Moby and *Swingers* star and creator John Favreau attended the low-key affair that lasted well into the night. By the time the boys woke up the next morning, their bags were packed and they were on the plane back to London for the all-important homecoming show at the London Forum. "We were in and out so fast, but we saw enough to know it's this huge, sprawling place with lots of different-looking people. Quite exciting but very, very different from Britain," said Buckland.

As 2000 drew to a close, the band had barely a moment to breathe and take in what had just happened to them. The first year of the new century had given the band so much: excitement, attention, fame, glory, admiration, stress, pressure, and, of course, the all-consuming angst and self-doubt. And more of it was on the way. During a reflective moment, Martin told Wendy Mitchell of *Billboard* magazine, "I'm sure when we all break for Christmas, hopefully we'll all be able to sit down and think about what went down this year; then we'll appreciate it more. And when the new year begins, I'll start pulling out my hair—or what's left of it."

If it has to come down to it we say, "Would U2 have done it? Would Radiohead have done it? Would Oasis have done it?" That answer always reinforces our decision. [Chris Martin]

The two-week tour, soft by rock 'n' roll standards, was meant to be a way to usher in Coldplay to these cities. The idea was to "underplay" those markets and make the tickets to these shows almost impossible to get. They could have easily filled venues twice the size, but it was the intention to leave each town they had just played wanting more. Unlike plenty of their fellow countrymen who face half-empty houses on stateside jaunts, Coldplay boldly sold out their first U.S. tour with ease.

Meanwhile, "Yellow" was having a field day at modern rock radio and you couldn't turn on MTV, or its sister station MTV2, without seeing a young Chris Martin sporting a windbreaker while lip-synching in the English rain. By the time Coldplay touched down in Seattle on February 9th, the song was entrenched in the Top 10 at modern rock and *Parachutes* was selling well over 20,000 records per week, breaking into the *Billboard* Top 200 sales chart at a respectable number 68. None of the boys seemed to mind the American attention as they watched it all happen from their homes in January. "It's crazy," Champion told a reporter for a Seattle newspaper. "We just sort of managed to get used to

what's gone on in England, and now it's all kicking off in America. We love what's happening, but it's difficult to come to grips with it." Knowing that "Yellow" was the sole reason for this overnight success in the States, even Martin didn't argue, saying to the same reporter, "How can you possibly complain about having a hit single? If somebody likes our song I don't care if it's a pope or a pauper. I want to shake each and every one of them by the hand and say, 'Good on you, you don't like Mariah Carey or the Baha Men, you like something good.' That's why it's important to keep ourselves in the limelight . . . because we've got a war to wage."

Before kicking off their North American tour, there was a "quick" stop in the land down under to take part in the annual Big Day Out festival circuit in Australia and New Zealand. Accepting this tour and accepting its routing by management proved to be a grave mistake. In the very first interview on the American tour, a satiated Chris Martin told Andy Savage of KNDD-FM in Seattle, "You know that book *Around the World in Eighty Days*? Well, we should write a book and call it *Around the World In Two Days*, cause that's what we've just done. We went from Australia to America by way of England . . . we took the long way." Buckland added in a defeated, monotone voice, "We just went around the world, you see. On Monday we were in Australia. Tuesday we were in the UK, Wednesday in Canada, and Thursday we're in America." "It's mad," said Martin. "We don't get to see any of it, mind you. We sleep a little, eat a little, and play a little." To make matters worse, the constant temperature changes had obviously compounded their already fragile state. And to add fuel to the growing fire, while most bands vacationed and chilled on the sunny beaches of Australia, management had Coldplay working, promoting, and ass-kissing their collective tails off during Big Day Out. Recalls Buckland, "We had just finished the Big Day Out run. It was a three-week tour. Most bands call it the Big Day Off tour 'cause you play your gigs on the Friday and Sunday of each week, then you get loaded, pick up girls, and go to the beach for the rest of the week." He continues, "But, man . . . not for us. We worked and we worked hard. A gig every night, an in-store, interviews, meet and greets . . . it was nonstop."

So, from the Big Day Out tour, the band hopped right on a plane from Sydney in the middle of summer to the dead of winter in the northwest of America. After the Vancouver gig in Canada, the band dropped anchor in the Seattle rain and all immediately proceeded to pick up a nasty flu bug . . . not to mention a case of the homesick blues. "We all knew 'Yellow' was happening and the record was starting to sell, but we couldn't even get to that place, you know," explains Martin. "We couldn't enjoy it. We had just come from the sun and now it was bloody cold and we had been working together, living together nonstop for what seemed like months and months."

Despite the turmoil, the sold-out American tour began. Seattle was the first stop and it was there that I met up with the band. After a shortened on-air acoustic set for KNDD (we, the record label, had told the station that Coldplay was going to do a six-song acoustic set for radio station winners, but the band called it quits after three songs), in which the program director, Phil Manning, glared over at me and said, "Three songs? Let's hope they play more [at the show] tonight," the band sat themselves down for yet another promotional obligation—the meet and greet with radio station winners and staff. It was here that I thought it best to get to know the band on more personal terms. We'd met during their trip to Los Angeles the past December, but it was so rushed for everyone that any concentrated or meaningful conversation was next to impossible. I thought I'd attempt to break the stiffness by saying casually to Chris, "I love the album. Not just the single. 'High Speed' . . . now that's *my* jam." While signing posters and CD jackets, Martin slowly lifted his tired head, looked me directly in the eye, and said, "Your *jam*? Is that some American record executive lingo? To try to sound cool or that you liken us to Pearl Jam?" His lips formed the makings of a smile, but not one that you would deem photo-worthy. It was a sarcastic smile at best; one that is meant to say, "Please . . . not now." I *was* being sincere and honest; I really did love that song. I tried to rebound from my feeble attempt at a connection with stories of success that Capitol Records was having with "Yellow" and the entire album, but all Chris could say back was, "That's great . . . but tell it to the other guys in the band. Make sure they know, too." What Martin was implying, besides not wanting to get into some meaningless chitchat with some record executive he didn't even know, was what had obviously been gnawing at the group for a while now. It happened in Australia and it was happening back home, as well; Coldplay was becoming colossal and it was the lead singer, and *just* the lead singer, who everyone wanted a piece of. It was the guy with the falsetto voice, the front man that the media was paying attention to, and this was starting to tear these four friends apart. Martin wanted anyone and everyone to know that this is not the Chris Martin Band; it's a four-piece rock group with equal power shared four ways and the group is called Coldplay. "Coldplay is a band. A group of four guys. We are a four-person democracy" is something that you started to hear quite a bit out of Martin during this tour. DJ of KNDD, Andy Savage even slipped at the end of the shortened interview and said, "I want to thank Chris Martin and the band for coming by and. . . ." Martin interrupted him, sarcastically saying, "Could you do us a favor and call us the Chris Martin Band? The guys would *really* love it if you did that." The spotlight was already shining too much on Martin and he wanted four lights, one for each band member, or none at all. During the same interview, Martin was asked what had been the greatest accomplishment in their young but prosperous careers thus far. After a long pause, Martin looked around the room, glanced over to his band mates, and answered the question with his head hanging down, saying, "To be honest . . . staying together is our greatest accomplishment. Staying together and trying to make new songs." This was

clearly a band on edge. Grand things were happening; countless opportunities that nine out of ten bands would be able only to dream about. The world could be Coldplay's for the taking, but as Martin alluded to, they "couldn't even get to that place."

The reviews during the first leg of this February 2001 tour were reviews that careers are made of. But again, they went virtually unnoticed by the members of the band. At The Show Box in Seattle, the *Seattle Weekly* said, "It's been a while since Seattle has witnessed a music phenomenon first-hand. Coldplay gives out the looming possibility that this could be their first step on a long, fruitful path." *Spin* was also in attendance, saying, "Bonus points for sounding better live than on record. The Show Box was a cauldron of hushed intimacy. The highlight of the evening by far was 'Yellow,' which the audience knew by heart." It was what Martin said before they played their smash single that spoke volumes; the before-song banter that put this current tour and the bands state into perspective. As Buckland went into the opening guitar lines of "Yellow," Martin stepped up to the microphone and said his now-infamous punchline. "This song is our meal ticket. Without it, we'd be on food stamps. I hope you enjoy our meal ticket." As the song kicked in the venue erupted, but it was a shame that the only ones in the entire building that "couldn't even get to that place" were the four guys onstage performing the song.

The next day in Portland would do the band some good. Some much-needed boost for their self-esteem would come from KNRK and its devoted audience. Before the show at the Roseland, Martin and Buckland were interviewed by the station.

I think I'm crap, which drives me. But I also think we're brilliant. That's the riddle. [Chris Martin]

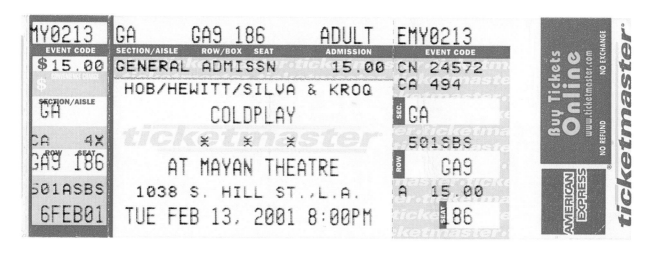

"Phil Harvey, our best mate and manager, has kept going on and on about your radio station. 'Just remember to thank KNRK when you see them. This station is the reason for everything in America,' " Martin said as they sat down for the interview. February 10th was indeed a distinctive night for Portland and Coldplay. A unique bond had been created between the band and the city, all thanks to KNRK. By the time the band rolled into town, the station had played "Yellow" over seven hundred times and now was onto "Shiver" and "Don't Panic." This was unheard of for a new band that has never played the market before, to have not only two songs on the playlist, but *three*! Before stepping one foot into the state of Oregon, Coldplay was already heralded as a very big band . . . one of Portland's own. The Roseland was packed, feverish, a sense of urgency in the air. This was to be an exceptional evening for everyone in attendance. Martin seemed to lighten up a bit during the radio interview and was able to clear his conscience on

several matters. "We might very well be a one hit wonder. But better to have one hit than none at all. At the end of the day, we are happy with the album. We think it's great and its not just a collection of some good songs, but a great album as a whole." He even alluded, for the first time, to some new material that seemed to rejuvenate the band's creative mojo. "We like *Parachutes*, but we can do better. There's a new song that we've been working on. It's the best thing we've ever done. This song is keeping us together right now." The song Martin was referring to was "In My Place." Some time later, Martin told *Q* magazine that, "After we recorded *Parachutes* we had one song left—'In My Place.' Apart from that I was dry. And I thought, That's it, we're done. But when Jonny played me his guitar part for the song, I thought, Well, we have to record that. It's the best thing we've ever written. And that was the song that saved us." The Roseland show was the first time they had ever played the song in a public forum. They unleashed it as their final song of the evening, right after "Yellow." "We already played our hit. This song will be a hit in about a year," said Martin before unveiling the midtempo rocker. Strong words, but even that night you could tell the band had new-found energy and the song gave them an immediate lift. "In My Place" left the crowd stunned; a perfect way to end such a heroic evening. The review in the *Oregonian* said, "From the cheers Coldplay received, there was no doubt that the night and the city of Portland belonged to the latest heirs to the Radiohead throne."

San Francisco was next and it was much of the same; it appeared as if things were picking up. Where it felt like the roof was caving in on them in Seattle, now the band was getting into a rhythm. Maybe America wasn't so "big and bad" after all; maybe this giant could be slayed. After a stellar on-air acoustic performance at the Bay Area's heritage and staple alternative rock station LIVE 105, the band played to an oversold audience at the world-famous Fillmore Auditorium. In the van ride to the venue from LIVE-105, the band had a lightness to them that had yet to be seen on this tour. They were generally excited to play on the same stage that has been graced by the likes of the Doors, the Grateful Dead, Jefferson Airplane, Cream, and Led Zeppelin. Martin opened the show by saying, "I think this is the most wicked place we've ever played," as the band launched into a haunting version of "Spies." "Coldplay Sizzles at Fillmore" read the *San Francisco Chronicle* headline the next day.

With no days off in between, the band rushed down California's long Highway 5 for two SRO nights at the Mayan Theater in downtown Los Angeles. The only stop on the tour with multiple nights, this was Coldplay's first trip back to L.A. since their triumphant visit two months prior. The band's attitude and karma were high and the anticipation and buzz around the band's arrival in Los Angeles was over the top. Things couldn't have been going any better now, until, of course, they *showed up*. Snow hit hard in the central California area, known as the grapevine, causing a seven-hour delay and turning what should have been a six-hour drive down the highway into a thirteen-hour hell ride. If the guys in the band weren't already ailing, by now they all had a bug of some sort . . . including a bug up all their respective asses. These were deeply unhappy people and the packed schedule of events in Tinseltown that Capitol Records and management had planned for them wasn't going to make it any easier to digest. They were able to curb their tempers for these crucial Los Angeles concerts and the reviews were glowing. World-renowned rock critic Robert Hilburn of the *Los Angeles Times* was sold. "Coldplay's music speaks of life in ways that carry the poetry of truth. The band accentuated the gentle optimism and intimacy of its songs with a decidedly understated, though never cold, delivery. A better name for the group might even be Warmplay." He gushed on. "At a time when so much U.S. commercial rock is taken up with paint-by-number anger and aggression, a band with its own voice and a down-to-earth approach is doubly rewarding. Coldplay makes music that comes from the heart, never contrived in the ways that encourage us to talk about movies and music as 'product.' " The reviews from all corners, fans, trade magazines, industry mouthpieces, and

Chapter 9

"Our Worst Gig Ever"

The band's return home was just what the doctor ordered. After taking home the prize for Album of the Year and New Artist of the Year at the 2001 Brit Awards, the band used the months of March, April, and May to play some headline dates in the UK, get their home life in order, and even take a holiday. Longing for any sort of privacy and relaxation was critical for Coldplay and even stepping out their own front doors was getting tough. "I'm more popular in my hometown than anywhere else now. Where it used to take me two minutes to go to the post office, it now takes over thirty minutes. It's strange. I don't mind it as much as my dog does. He just wants to go home," laughs Buckland. "I was walking down the street, and I walked past these two girls, and one of them whispered, 'That's the bass player from Coldplay' . . . it was so weird," says Berryman.

The band owed America some makeup dates. Most notable were New York and Boston. They had to get back to the States to do some gigs in the summer, so it was decided by management and record label (I, unfortunately, had a major hand in this one) to use the summer of 2001 to play the radio festival circuit in America. These radio station summer shows were as rudimentary as anything now. Major summer festivals such as Lollapalooza, Horde, Lillith Fair, and Womad were past tense. No major summer tours made sense for Coldplay, as the annual OzzFest and Warped Tours did not match, so it was up to the radio stations and their respective festivals to get Coldplay back on its feet and back in the good graces of the American public. As Martin saw it, "It was weird playing in football stadiums with the likes of Limp Bizkit and Linkin Park. Completely out of place. It was like, 'Hang on, let's do it. Let's at least try to win everyone over. Everyone.' " Coldplay needed their biggest fan base possible, so it was decided that they take part in the following radio station sponsored festivals: The WBCN River Rave in Boston at Foxboro Stadium, home to the NFL New England Patriots; the WHFS-sponsored HFStival at D.C.'s downtown RFK Stadium, past home of the Washington Redskins; and the king of them all, the KROQ Weenie Roast at Irvine Meadows, just south of Los Angeles. The problem was the bands booked for these three extravaganzas were bands that fit the hard-edge sound of the times. Bands that liked to play fast, loud, dumb, and angry. These were rock shows designed with a capital R and the audience came to these shows wanting to *rock*.

"We were put on these shows to open for bands like Blink 182 and Linkin Park, and being that we were the only act with songs under one hundred bpm, it was a challenge to win over the crowd," says Buckland. "They'd all come to drink, body surf, and hit each other. Our record company assured us that the flying objects were a sign that the crowd liked us, but I'm not sure I entirely believe that. A guy in the band before us in D.C. got his nose broken by a cell phone that hit him in the face. To be honest, I wasn't worried about my playing; I was worried about the flying bottles of piss."

Coldplay touched down in America for the second time in their young career on May 24th, Memorial Day weekend. First up was a makeup date in New York for the Irving Plaza show they had canceled back in February. The show, moved to the Roseland Ballroom, double the size of Irving Plaza, sold out in minutes, but *The New York Times* gave the band a less-than-favorable review of their performance. "Though the band's musical chemistry was tight, its personal chemistry was not. The rest of the band members did not seem to like Mr. Martin at all. When he made his usual insecure jokes with the audience, they grimaced; when he accidentally hit his lip with the microphone at the end of 'Yellow', they smirked in delight." This high-profile opener to the new leg of the American tour was not the best way to start and things were beginning to speed downhill. It was time to play the 55,000-seat Foxboro Stadium for the WBCN River Rave. Hooking up with Chris Martin backstage, I felt a new source of tension and paranoia coming from him that only added to the mound of self-doubt that covered him on their last trip. While on their tour bus backstage, Martin shared some news that the band was going through for the first time; negative press and a wave of criticism from their backyard. Britain loves nothing more, especially the music tabloids, than to bring down someone who sits on a throne. They had just survived and defeated the Alan McGee/"bed wetter" episode, but this was new repercussion now coming from multiple mediums. "To be honest, I feel a real back-lash in Britain, and I feel like America's the only place that accepts us. I think we've sold too many records, so we're no longer cool in Britain." He began to rub his newly shaved head, almost Billy Corgan and Michael Stipe bald, and said, "If you're a middle-class boy with a guitar, you've got it coming, no matter how good your songs are." With that, Coldplay strolled out of the bus at 2:00 P.M., squinted their English eyes at the glaring New England sun, and walked onto the stadium stage. Jonny Buckland was right; these 55,000 strong came to riot. During Coldplay's near life-threatening set, I myself saw everything from water bottles and beer cans to hats, shirts, shoes, and boots heaved at Coldplay. I even saw some pizza land next to Martin's piano bench. This, on a sweltering, humid New England summer day, was not what Coldplay had in mind. The band, like true professionals, made their way through the performance and man-aged to dodge everything being cast their way. Adding new, never-before-heard songs such as "God Put a Smile Upon Your Face" and "In My Place" to their set list didn't help matters, either. After a lukewarm response to "Yellow" (at least, during the song, the crowd seemed to refrain from their game of "bottle toss"), Coldplay had put in their work for the day. They escaped the stage and retreated to their tour bus. Martin was the only one to stay behind for the already agreed-to aftershow interview with host radio station WBCN. This inter-view was one for the ages and Martin was in rare

form. Melissa and Bill Abott were the lucky DJs on hand for this no-holds-barred Q&A. Asked what it was like to play in front of 55,000 people, Martin replied, "Imagine being stroked by some nice young lady and then imagine being beaten by some three hundred-pound thug. That's what today was like. I don't even understand why you are even interviewing us 'cause we should just get out of here." When Bill Abott said the show was great and that Martin had nothing to worry about, Martin shot back, "Were you even there? Did you see the same show that I just saw? We have done about two hundred concerts and that had to be the worst reception we've *ever* had. Whoever booked us has got to be in trouble for this one." Martin's head turned in my direction and all I could do was stare at the station's program director, Oedipus, who kept his professional grin on throughout the interview. Melissa was next up, sharing her love and devotion for Coldplay. Melissa told Martin that *Parachutes* was her favorite album of the year and it was the band she was looking forward to seeing on the bill. "Oh, well . . . sorry. I mean, we were getting bottles thrown at us, man. I never have

been in so much pain for that long of a time onstage before." Much to the DJ's credit, Melissa and Bill Abott would not give up and eventually Martin warmed a little. He figured it couldn't get any worse and it's no use making enemies of the one medium that seems to be supporting his band in this town . . . the radio station. As the interview wrapped up, Martin was even able to joke about it. "I think that had to be the funniest half hour I've ever had in my life. It was like putting on a poodle show in the middle of a Texas rodeo." He closed by saying, "Thanks for having us . . . it was very brave of you guys. I mean, I think we're the best band in the world, but fifty-five thousand people in Boston seemed to disagree."

Washington, D.C. and the famed HFStival was next up; this time, though, it was 65,000 fans, 10,000 more than the previous day. Coldplay had to share the stage with the likes of Limp Bizkit, Linkin Park, Blink 182, and Godsmack. "We're beyond humble now," were the only words bass player Berryman was able to muster after the show. Later the next year, Martin had a chance to look back at that Memorial Day weekend spent on the East Coast. "I thought we had it. That we were done with. The British press had begun their attack and now water bottles were being chucked at us in America. When we came over to America for those shows, we thought, Great, we're going to a place where they love us, 'cause they sure don't love us at home anymore. But after those shows, the band, especially me, was considering packing the whole thing in. The bottom for us. Our worst gig ever." Coldplay was on the verge of the unthinkable; they were on the verge of breaking up. On pins and needles, Coldplay was actually debating whether to call it

a day and miss out on their place in music history. The band needed a shot of moral and self-assurance quick, and that timely gift would arrive at their next stop on the tour by way of Atlanta, Georgia.

"Atlanta turned things around . . . and turned them around good. Playing at this beautiful venue and playing 'Georgia on My Mind' was such a position turnaround. We felt like a band again," says Martin. The Atlanta show two days later, at the Tabernacle, was indeed a critical turning point. Where only four days earlier Coldplay had played "their worst gig ever," this Atlanta show rocketed right to the top of their all-time great performances. "Georgia on My Mind" was indeed a moment to remember, but every song has its "moment." From the opener "Spies" to "Trouble" to "Everything's Not Lost," this show was one knockout punch after another. Even

the new songs "God Put a Smile Upon Your Face" and "In My Place" went over well. Coldplay played with enough pent-up energy and raw passion for the roof of the Tabernacle to come right off. This was a concert that not only could keep a group together but take them to the next level. The group, as an act of solidarity, wore matching shirts and played their most passionate and intense set of their tour. "That was our best show in a long long time," remembers Berryman. "We knew then and there that we have fans and those are the ones we need to cater to." "We realized that we're lucky to have each other. Whoever we come into contact with, we're all protected by the other three, so there's no real danger. We're like the Mighty Morphin Power Rangers. They're all pretty good individually, but together they make a Mighty Morpher," decided Martin.

"We love these songs," says Champion. "We wrote them and are proud of them, and to belittle them in front of thousands hurts the credibility of the music." He continues, "It's all right to joke, don't get me wrong, but it was our songs that were the butt of it all. After a while, when Chris would do that, it started to affect how we played them, too."

So when they objected to Martin's apologizing, Martin agreed to stop degrading the song in public. Though the song struck a passionate chord with the public, Martin remained skeptical about its chance for success . . . especially in America. Anger and angst, even if manufactured and stale, was still the norm in the rock music world and Martin saw "Trouble" as a reason for the band to be an easy target. Still recovering from having water bottles tossed at him onstage in Boston and Washington, D.C., only fueled his temperament.

"Trouble" came to Martin on one of those painful days of the *Parachutes* sessions. After a fight, one of many with producer Ken Nelson, Martin retreated to one of the smallest rooms in the recording studio to hide and be alone. "There must have been something magical in that cupboard of a room because this lovely tune came out. I went right to the band with it and we suddenly started jamming on it . . . we struggled with the recording of it, but it turned out just great."

As the band's second single "Shiver" was winding down and fading fast on American radio, KROQ in Los Angeles quietly added "Trouble" to their playlist. *Parachutes* had already gone gold in the States (500,000 units sold), a respectable achievement and certainly one to build on for the next record. They had left the country after some great end-of-tour gigs in Atlanta and Los Angeles and were not expected to return until 2002. Capitol called it a day on the project, publicly calling *Parachutes* a tremendous success and a great battle won. Gold records were pressed and given to radio stations, record stores, and company employees. On the outside it appeared that Capitol was more than thrilled with their results, but it was clear to those on the inside that Coldplay was perceived as nothing more than a one-hit wonder; in quiet circles they were referred to as "the Yellow Band." Capitol was able to break a song, but not a band. That KROQ had added "Trouble" barely registered at the label. There was a sense at Capitol that it would be easier if the band just kind of went away to begin the process of a next record so the label could move on to other things. But as cream will rise to the top, the song was doing some climbing of its own. The domino effect was taking place. Next up was 99X in Atlanta, then 91X in San Diego, KNDD in Seattle, followed by KDGE in Dallas, and so on. This down-tempo ballad, driven by an unforgettable piano hook, was clearly breaking through the murky mud and swamp of the hard-edge music that alternative radio had become so synonymous with. Remembers program director of 99X in Atlanta Leslie Fram, "The song just stood out on the station. We didn't care if the

COLDPLAY
SAN DIEGO
8th December 2001

SHIVER

IN MY PLACE

DON'T PANIC

YELLOW

GOD PUT A SMILE...

TROUBLE

LOST HIGHWAY

SEE YOU SOON

audience wasn't ready for it. The band had such a buzz about them after the Tabernacle show and this was the song that we knew would break Coldplay." 91X in San Diego PD Bryan Shock seconds the motion. "I remember 'Trouble' from the time I got the advance copy of the record. We didn't care if the label was working it or not. We were going to play this song sooner or later."

Fame is bullshit. But there are moments when I have even thought, You lucky bastard. Enjoy it. [Chris Martin]

Much to the surprise of Capitol, who by this time, with the exception of a few holdovers (myself included), had an entirely new regime on board, "Trouble" was becoming a bona fide radio hit. A new president, a new general manager, a new head of Promotion, and a whole new set of priorities and agendas almost caused the label to miss this moment. Matters got even better when the band delivered the video to MTV. Remembers Holmes, "The band was reluctant to even do a video for the song. They had enough of *Parachutes* and were itching to record their next record . . . couldn't wait. But radio was telling us we had a hit and that finally convinced the band to do it." The video, a black-and-white, partly animated masterpiece that follows the band on an old convertible caboose moving slowly along a rusty train track, went right into what MTV calls "breakthrough rotation." At a time when every video being played on MTV's main channel was a multicolor, multilayered, overdone, pop culture extravaganza, Coldplay delivered a sparse, dark, and beautiful stunner that captured the fervor of the song. This breakthrough rotation was the frosting on the cake; soon enough,

sales for *Parachutes* kicked in again and Capitol had another Coldplay hit on their hands. America was calling for Coldplay to return for a three-week run, in September and October of 2001, that would cover much of the South and Eastern parts of the U.S. "Coldplay was ready to pack it in and not return to America for a long time," said Holmes. "But the demand was really picking up for the band . . . everyone wanted a piece of them. Then came the terrible events of 9/11."

"We were home and I remember sitting, eating a sandwich, when all of the sudden I got a call from Guy, who was at a pub down the street from me. He told me to turn on the telly and what I saw changed my life," recalls Martin. "The one thing that I immediately remember thinking was, I've got to be with my friends right now, my mates. I really needed to be with the band." Needless to say, the band canceled the tour of the States, but an array of new emotions and song ideas came to Martin and the rest of the band. Many of the new songs, including "Politix," were a direct result of the events of 9/11. In interviews, Martin will say "Politix" is an "ode" to 9/11 and how life cannot be taken for granted. "I wrote the song on 9/11 and we recorded it on 9/13. We were all, like everyone else I suppose, a little confused and frightened," he says. "I get off tour and had a rest for one or two days, but then I get antsy again. I want to write songs and do things, 'cause you never know what might happen. You got to live in the moment. Now there's not a single day where I don't think, Ah, it could be the end today. And I don't mean that in a morbid way. I never had people I knew die, or I'd never been somewhere where there was a disaster. That realization of mortality just makes you sort of clear out

all the junk and think about what's important. It
just kick-starts you, really." As it did for millions,
9/11 forever altered the way Coldplay looked at the
world. "Pointless things became just that. We're
just musicians in a band. What we do is really so
insignificant in the grand scheme of things. We
have to always think about bigger issues and the
cause and effect of things," says Martin. Coldplay
was growing up and the events of 9/11 only fueled
their maturation. Martin did have a positive spin
on his responsibility and influence as a rock star,
saying, "I mean, if our music makes people feel
good . . . if it touches them and moves them, then
I'm all for doing what we do. If we can provide that
to people as a source of healing then I want to
continue . . . then, yes, I love my job."

As September turned into October and then
November, it was Christmas show time once again
for American radio stations. It was just the previous
year when Coldplay got its jump-start in America
by playing KROQ's Almost Acoustic 2000 bill. The
annual Christmas shows put on by radio are decidedly more low-key affairs than the summer outdoor
festivals. In keeping with the holiday and winter
spirit, these shows are toned down, more sedate;
the venues are smaller and the number of bands are
downsized, making for a more intimate experience.
This vibe fits Coldplay to a tee. They had had such
a great experience with the KROQ show the
previous year that they agreed to do a series of
them to wrap up 2001. Martin called me in early
November from the recording studio, saying that
the band wanted to end 2001 in America on a high
note and play some radio-sponsored shows. "We
want to thank radio for supporting [us] when maybe
they didn't have to." Capitol jumped at the chance

to have the band back and covered the costs for
a week-long run of dates. They included WHFS
Washington, D.C., WBRU Providence, KNDD
Seattle, 91X San Diego, closing out with the station
responsible for carrying the "Trouble" torch, KROQ
Los Angeles. The shows were a remarkable sendoff
for the band, the perfect finale for a stellar year. At
each stop they stole the show. In D.C. they played
before System of a Down. Six months prior, this
would have filled the band with panic. Pat Ferrise,
music director of WHFS, said at the time, "You can
tell how much confidence Chris Martin has now.
The whole band, for that matter. Such a change
from when they played our festival this past
summer." In Seattle, Coldplay played with multiplatinum angst rockers Staind and easily held their
own. KNDD Program Director Phil Manning, who
loved their show, was even more impressed with
their demeanor backstage, saying, "It's as if they
got rid of the monkey they were carrying on their
backs. The band has a swagger now. . . . a complete
one-eighty from last time." And reviewing the
KROQ show in Los Angeles, trade magazine *HITS*
said, "Artist Development Story of 2001. Coldplay.
If you had the opportunity to see them play at
KROQ's Almost Acoustic Christmas show this past

Martin defends his right to crusade. "We kept getting asked to give our music to commercials and advertisements for huge sums of money and we really never want to do that. Instead of advertising a pair of shoes or breakfast cereal, why don't we advertise what we care about. Oxfam approached us to become part of the Make Trade Fair project and I was convinced to crusade for it after I went to Haiti and saw what big companies and international trade regulators get away with. The arrogant exploitation that they all get away with is just horrific. One of the biggest causes of poverty around the world is the fact that trade laws are all wrong and very unbalanced. Our job is just to advertise this website and this idea of addressing trade laws. You know, celebrities always use their position to advertise things, so why shouldn't we? Look at everyone advertising Gap or Starbucks or whatever.

It's fucking bollocks, man. We're not selling a product and we're not preaching It's something we believe in. Of course, it's rock star conscience. I mean, I am loaded. And I love my life. And I'm selfish. But I've woken up to the shit underneath. When you realize that there are rules keeping people in poverty because they're not allowed to trade, you wake up."

Guy, Jonny, and Wil came to Los Angeles to take part in the 2002 Grammy Awards. Coldplay was nominated for Alternative Album of the Year, up against heavyweights Beck and the previous year's winner, Radiohead. "We don't care about awards or award shows . . . unless we don't win," said a relaxed Champion as they hopped into a limousine to take them to the Staples Center for the evening's show. For the first time, they were in America to relax . . . some drinking, some partying, some California sunshine. When it was announced that they had won the Grammy, it just made their celebration that much sweeter. I was able to nab the one empty seat in the bands' limousine that was en route to the EMI post-Grammy party. The three mates were at ease and ready to let their hair down. It was on the way to the party where I was treated to some tracks from the forthcoming album. Berryman put a cassette into the stereo and what I heard was inspiring, intense, and miles ahead of what I expected. They played me rough tracks of "Daylight," "In My Place," "The Scientist," and "God Put a Smile Upon Your Face." Unfinished, but yes,

already clearly leaps and bounds ahead of what *Parachutes* had given us. This was going to be a big record . . . something rare, something extraordinary. The boys spent the evening hobnobbing with the likes of Thom Yorke, Radiohead and Travis producer Nigel Goodrich, Beck, Aussie rockers the Vines, and Lisa Marie Presley. The three had an air, an aura about them that evening, as if they knew they were sitting on something that was going to be momentous and groundbreaking. When word of the Grammy Award got back to Martin, all he could think about was the new album. "We are so desperate to record, to get back in the studio and make some new songs," he said. "We can't wait to have a go at it."

Control Room

A.I.R.
Studio 1

Mic

Booth

Control Room

Booth

Booth

Booth

Parr Street
Studio 3

Chapter 12

"In Our Place"

"We were like cultural sponges during these last two years of touring and promoting around *Parachutes*," Martin says. "We've just discovered so much new music and new places and new people and new friends and we just wanted to sort of spew some of that out, you know? Everything from Johnny Cash to the Streets to Echo and the Bunnymen, the Cure, and all these things, then meeting people like PJ Harvey, and everyone from Fred Durst to Bono . . . and all this just goes in your head, and we were really, really, really desperate to do something different."

In January 2002, *Billboard* magazine asked Martin what could be expected from the next record. *Parachutes* had been a platinum seller in over a dozen countries, amassed an armful of awards and accolades, and the pressure was high for the band to top it. Flush with the promise of a beautiful future, the band had already created a definitive pop formula; introspective lyrics, visceral melodies, and sentient guitar-based rock. Could they make it work twice? Martin's answer to the question revealed not the pressure they felt from the industry and fans of *Parachutes*, but the pressures they felt from themselves to make a great album. "We want to be the best band of all time. I just want to make the best music of all time with my best friends. In my head, we compete with U2 and the Beatles, so in that sense, we're trying to make the most soulful record ever made. I want us to be the biggest, best band in the fucking world and we're gonna keep trying and trying until we get there." Only on their second album and already Coldplay had to gear up for their career-defining record. "It's like a big *Rocky*-style challenge for us as a band. We're not going to be scared of anyone anymore."

The recording of *A Rush of Blood to the Head* had begun in the early winter of 2001. "We wanted to go in and make an album that will be catchy without being slick, poppy without being pop, and uplifting without being pompous," stated Martin. During the surprising success that the track "Trouble" was having in the States and at home (where it had just cracked into the Top 10 on the British charts), Coldplay finally bunkered down in central London's Mayfair Studios. "Mayfair is a lovely studio, and it's really close to where we all live," recalls Buckland. "But we weren't particularly focused when we were there because it was the first time we'd been back and seeing our friends." With a lack of concentration and sense that they were simply going through the motions, Coldplay laid down an album's worth of material, but upon returning from America each had empty feelings about the Mayfair recording. There was a general perception that many of the songs felt contrived, forced. "We all kinda went, 'Ahhh, shit,' " recalls Champion. "I mean, the songs were good, but just not good enough for what we were wanting to do. Everyone says that second albums are always shite, and we were determined to make this one ace. We could have just made a half-arsed second album and sort of trotted through it and said, 'Oh, we'll make a good one next time.' But this is our big chance and we decided to put everything into this. At the end of the day, even if you think it's shite, it's not as shite as it could've been." Having spent more hours in the local pubs than inside the studio, the guys were longing for more innocent times and chose to return to Parr Street Studios in Liverpool, site of the *Parachute* sessions. "We moved to Parr Street for a couple of months to their smallest studio, which has a tiny little desk, but a lovely little room. We brought in some of our own equipment and ended up writing more than half the album there," claims Buckland. "Parr Street has this homey vibe for us that became *so* important as the pressure was beginning to mount," states Champion. Remembers Martin, "When we went back to Liverpool it was like a big liberation; we were completely away from any distractions. We had complete freedom to write, play, and sing however we wanted, while not worrying about pressure of record sales, critics, the business, or whatever. And it was cheap, too."

Once settled, Coldplay began re-recording the songs, such as "God Put a Smile . . ." and "Politix" that had been lacking the inspiration and the vigor they were seeking. Martin even took up singing lessons to sharpen his vocal technique and stamina. "It gives me such a buzz singing now and everyone always looks at me a bit weird when I tell them I'm taking lessons, ya know. But I've got so much better and now I feel like I know what I'm doing. I'm nearly as good as Celine Dion now," he joked. In addition, Martin began writing new songs at a prolific clip. "We wanted to maintain the emphasis on melody and emotion. Apart from that, we wanted to do whatever was coming naturally," explains Martin. "We'd be working on something and Chris would go in the other room and just bash out something on the piano and come and say, like, 'Guys, I've got this. What do you think?' " recalls Berryman. "And we'd put that track down and then start working on it straight away. It wasn't forced and it felt like we were onto something very special each time." Songs that were originated, written, and recorded during their extended stay in Liverpool included "Daylight," "A Whisper," and "Clocks." "We were listening to a lot of Echo [and the Bunnymen] and the Cure and things with a bite to them at the time. And I think it showed during our time at Parr Street; the new songs had a bit of edge to them," reflects Martin.

The band left the Parr Street experience feeling at ease and unshackled for the first time in months. They decided to finish up the record at the famous Sir George Martin–owned A.I.R. recording studio back in London. With some songs in the can and all basic tracks laid down to tape, panic struck once again as the band's self-imposed deadline to finish the record had come and gone. Things seemed to

flow a little too much on the natural side in Liverpool and a suspicious Martin quipped, "My theory is that every record should be difficult to make . . . if you truly care about it." Later, he told *Q* magazine, "The danger was we'd make a half-arsed, shitty, bargain-bin, average, follow-up record with songs not half as good as 'Yellow.' I'm not interested in, 'Here are some off-cuts of the first album and I've got loads of money and coke and I'm in *OK!* magazine.' That's bullshit." Misery always needs company so, on top of the missed deadline, came a series of tabloid-driven rumors that this was to be the last Coldplay album; breakup rumors abounded. Martin had his words taken out of context and overblown when NME.com reported in the spring of 2002 that after "Coldplay releases the upcoming *A Rush of Blood to the Head*, the band is set to call it quits." Martin, quickly dispensing damage control, responded to the scuttlebutt by saying, "All I said was maybe this'll be our last record. What I meant was, I don't care about our next record or our fifth record. None of us do. We only care about this one. It's about now. Put everything into it now. My granddad always said, 'Do it now. Don't put things off and worry about what might happen.' " Champion came to the defense, saying, "It's the only healthy way to think. I'd hate to think that in five years' time, our fourth album or something, and thinking, Ah, this is quite good; it's not as good as the last one, but it'll do. That's the kind of complacency that we hope to God that we never get to that point. The only kind of criteria that we judge an album on is if we really sincerely believe that it is an improvement or a progression. There's no point in just resting on our laurels and stagnating as a band. We have to keep to ourselves to keep interested and to keep other people interested."

The listening party was held on a rare sunny Saturday afternoon, April 12th, at A.I.R. The studio, where Coldplay was currently holed up, was decorated with candles, dim lighting, fluffy pillows, beanbag chairs, and soft couches to create the right listening atmosphere for the guests. While everyone was escorted into the room as they sipped on tea and coffee and ate finger sandwiches, there was panic and chaos in the studio control room.

Members of the band, band management, their producer Ken Nelson, and both presidents of Capitol and Parlaphone had been huddled there for over an hour. "They were just kind of suffocating in the studio. The self-imposed deadline they put on themselves was putting way too much pressure on the guys," said managing director of Parlaphone UK Keith Wozencroft. This was supposed to be a classy and unforgettable album listening party, but there was a significant ingredient missing . . . *the music.* The new record wasn't finished, not by a long shot. What had become common practice in the Coldplay camp had repeated itself; as with *Parachutes*, the band was once again behind schedule. They hadn't come close to completing the album and, while agonizing over the decision to delay the pending release date or not, waited until their guests from overseas arrived to share the news. "This," sighed friend and comanager Phil Harvey, "is what happens when art and marketing collide." After some fingernail biting and last-second maneuvering, it was decided that Coldplay would premier four songs to their now-anxious guests. "The natives are getting restless," said manager Holmes. "We have to give them something. I mean, we have guests who flew all

the way over from America to hear some new songs and we can't leave them empty-handed." The band acquiesced and after an hour of eating appetizers and drinking cold coffee, visitors were treated to "Daylight," "The Scientist," "Politix," and "In My Place." Lights went down and eyes were closed as the new music pumped through the immaculate A.I.R. studio sound system. At the end of "In My Place," one of the programmers stood up and demanded an encore . . . he was not alone. "In My Place" was played a second time, as Chris, Guy, Jonny, and Wil made their grand entrance from the control room. Never one to disappoint, Martin apologized to the group for the delay, for the fighting that went on in the control room, for the lack of warm drinks, for the beanbag chairs, for his hair allegedly falling out, for the weather, and for only playing four songs. But it didn't matter. Everyone was in awe and blown away as the music they had heard only whet their appetites for more. Another "brilliant mistake" from Coldplay as everyone made their way out of the A.I.R. complex; "Remember, always leave your audience wanting more," said a grinning Martin. Despite the tension, the delays, and the duress of the lengthy recording process, this was a clear victory;

the buzz was, once again, officially rolling. "Coldplay is making music that will put them on a level that no other current band will be able to touch. A league of their own," said music director of WPLY Philadelphia Dan Fein. "That was unbelievable. When can we get a copy of this? I want to put this right on the air," said an ecstatic Mary Shuminas, music director of WKQX Chicago.

Word of mouth was traveling fast; almost overnight, as American radio and the music industry had gotten wind about the four songs that Coldplay debuted.

As the Capitol executives landed back in the States, marketing plans were now on their way for the launching of the new record with its sharp new title of *A Rush of Blood to the Head*. This was not going to be your typical release plan; a worldwide assault was being readied. The following Monday, the band formally announced that they would be headlining two high-profile festivals in England. The first, the David Bowie–organized Meltdown Festival, of which Coldplay was at the very top of Bowie's wish list to appear, and second, the Glastonbury Festival. Headlining the pyramid stage at "Glasto" had been a dream since they first played on the new stage at the 1999 event and their wishes had now been granted. "We want to use this show as a first step. Headlining Glastonbury, to us, is like Radio City Music Hall times ten. It's where we grew up and it means everything to us to headline the festival," said Martin.

The Meltdown show took place at London's Royal Festival Hall. A 2,000-seater, now considered a smaller-size venue for a band with Coldplay's stature,

it was overfilled and when the band struck up the first chords of "Yellow," hundreds of fans sprang up from their seats and rushed the front of the low stage. It was obvious that the Royal Festival Hall, and venues like it, had become too cozy for the band and many in the audience felt that this would be the last time they would see Coldplay in this type of intimate setting. The Glastonbury headline spot, in late June, was an entirely different setting; *NME* magazine was on hand to tell the tale. "Ten past midnight on Friday on the pyramid stage was the exact point when Coldplay made their claim to greatness. 'In My Place,' their new single, pushed them to a whole different level. Mournful, tender, and with a plangent guitar riff so classic sounding it seemed to have been around a hundred years, it was like an anthem for the whole festival. 'In My Place' was the culmination of a set which showed exactly how far Coldplay has come; bed wetters no more, they're now soul-stirring practitioners of the Big Music. They did us—and themselves—proud." A slew of other magazines and tabloids were on hand to cover this historic and star-making performance. Gossip rag *Star* said, "Coldplay took the baton passed down from Radiohead on Friday night. Their super set including hits 'Yellow' and 'Trouble' wooed the audience until Glastonbury was a sea of contentment." The *Guardian* offered up this observation: "The closest the weekend came to a classic set was Coldplay's Friday night pyramid stage bill-topper. Two years ago they were languishing in the middle of the afternoon on the side stage, but here they came of age before your eyes. During 'Trouble,' the hushed, high-pitched mass contribution almost brought a tear to the eyes of front man Chris Martin, causing him to say, 'Best choir I ever heard in my life.'"

Chapter 14

A Rush of Coldplay to the World—the Album and Band Is Unleashed

"Five months ago, I remember sitting in Devon with my parents and thinking, Shit, we'll never finish this album. We'll never get it to sound how we want it to sound. Even now, I refuse to believe we've finished it," Martin said, shaking his head in exhaustion. Ten months and eleven songs later . ten months of tweaking the guitar lines and overanalyzing every possible drum and cymbal, ten months of vocal takes and three recording studios later, *A Rush of Blood to the Head* could not be edited, polished, shined, or redone anymore. Some three hundred days after they had begun this process, the band members emerged from the confines of the studio looking like zombies. From the wrinkled shirts and wine-stained pants, way past the five o'clock shadow and now onto major facial stubble, the boys appeared spent.

The behind-the-music story did not include totaling sports cars, wrecking hotel rooms, sleeping with supermodels, or fighting drug addictions; it is the story of eleven perfectly crafted, statement- and genre-defining songs all worked on with feverish intensity. They took this seriously and the proof was on the wax, or rather, the disc. There were countless nights of restless sleep, bolting up and wanting desperately to get back to work on melodies, bridges, snare-drum sounds, or whatever was causing them to lose precious and hard-earned REM sleep. "You know, I don't have to worry about working in a mine or looking after my ten kids. This job I've been given, this privilege, allows me to be obsessed with the middle eight of a song. And it's amazingly cool to be able to be that geeky about something. We care so deeply about our music . . . about recording. I know it's unhip, but I love getting the hi-hat sound just right," said a proud Martin.

"It's like trying to analyze your own nose. We became totally, utterly obsessed with this record. Now it's finished, and I don't know what we're supposed to think of it," he continued. The album's title, *A Rush of Blood to the Head*, is a British expression that serves as a timely metaphor for being alive, living in the present, and being in tune with the adrenaline of the moment. When asked what the new album was "about," Martin offered this explanation; "Let's see . . . it's what every album's about. Your fear of death, your love of girls, and your anger at the shit that politicians talk." He smiled then concluded with, "Mainly about girls, though. You might like George Bush or you might not, but the whole girl-boy thing? That's quite universal. It's kind of a unifying topic, isn't it?" He gave *Q* magazine a more somber answer when he said, "My best songs come when I have that feeling that I've left the party early. And the other reason these songs are about struggling and worrying and being beleaguered is because of my dad. He's a terrible worrier. He's always after the next thing. And I am, too. Luckily, the other members are more relaxed. Three other members like me and we'd go nuts." It took ten months, but the eleven songs that were hatched and cared for came from a strict desire to get it right and they would spare no mental or physical expense to achieve this. With press interview after interview, the tension only seemed to mount for Martin. "Now I know why I'm in such a bad mood. Being asked if I feel any pressure fifteen times a day. I didn't. Now I do. I feel like our album's flopped and it hasn't even come out yet," Martin told *NME* right before the album's release.

Chris Martin, Track by Track

Politix	"We wanted a song where we just hit our instruments as loudly as possible and dispensed with the idea of fragility. Not to waste the potential missed opportunity of living in the now."
	This song has become the band's official opening piece during every concert they have played during their 2002–2003 world tour. Berryman adds, "There is only one place for 'Politix.' We could not have put this song in any other position than number one and there is no better song than this one to open our show."
In My Place	"That's about where you're put in the world, and how you're given your position, and the way you look and how you have to get on with it. We are not a singles band, but we knew this was to be the album's first single."
	The song, which sounds effortless, was actually one of the hardest to record. "This was the most problematic song we did for the album. About one hundred different versions were done and eventually we settled on the one that's on the record. But we wanted to get it right, 'cause we felt this was the song that made us come out of our shell . . . a bit more bold and a bit more confident," claims Champion.
God Put a Smile Upon Your Face	"This song came out of playing live and wanting to have a bit more bounce. We were really getting into things like PJ Harvey and a band called Muse . . . things with a bit more energy. It's about being lucky to be in such a great band."
The Scientist	"Well, it's about girls. It's weird, whatever else is on your mind, whether it's the downfall of global economics or environmental troubles, the thing that always gets you the most is when you fancy someone. This one became the turning point of the record for us. We wanted a piano ballad with layers of guitars. We wanted to see how pretty and how edgy we can get all in one song."

Clocks	We recorded this song very, very fast. Our newest song of the album and it came out really fresh. It was the creeper off this album. It really grew on us. Another one inspired by the band Muse."
Daylight	"Another one that was recorded very fast. It belonged next to 'Clocks.' We wouldn't have had it any other way. This was written in Liverpool and I don't know where it came from, but we are so very lucky to have this one."
Green Eyes	"It's about an American friend of mine who looked after me when I was being a bit of an idiot. I met this friend in New Mexico; I was out there to see a Dave Matthews concert and I'm glad I went to that concert and I'm glad I met her."
Warning Sign	"It's just a silly song about a girl. It's the one that I am now the furthest away from out of all the songs on this album."
	(Early on, "Warning Sign" was a contender for a second single choice to follow up "In My Place." When recently asked about "Warning Sign," Martin just first looked away and said, "I want nothing to do with that song. I won't play it and for all I care, it doesn't really exist.")
A Whisper	"This is also from the Liverpool sessions. No one really likes this song, but we put it on because of a very nerdy, technical thing that we did with the synthesizer sound. This one won the award for 'most likely to have been a B-side.' "
A Rush of Blood to the Head	"An homage to Johnny Cash, the greatest. Cash, Dylan, and Hank Williams are just the greatest men with guitars. And I really, really wanted to sing a song in this low key."
Amsterdam	"It's weird how this song made it on to the album. It never had that much attention paid to it. It's the simplest song of the eleven, but it took the longest to write. It was written in Amsterdam and it's a great one to close the record on."

With *A Rush of Blood to the Head* mastered, done, and out of the band's nervous hands, it was time for the public to hear the fruits of their labor. As the band readied themselves after their headlining gigs at Meltdown and Glastonbury, glowing and starry-eyed reviews of galactic proportions were coming in from every corner. The journalists taking to the band was a record label's wet dream. The label's very own Publicity department couldn't have written them better if they tried. Here are some samples:

Spin: "Two years ago, they were just a bunch of sweet guys with a Brit-pop dream. Then their song 'Yellow' became a massive hit and soon they were fending off rumors of megalomania. But now, Coldplay don't mind; they've just made the greatest album ever."

Rolling Stone: "The rush of blood and hope on this record seals it. Coldplay are our new U2."

I would go hide in the bathroom and read about U2, and my friend and I would think about being a band like that some day. The whole idea was so unlikely that the story is hysterical. [Chris Martin]

USA Today: "Coldplay moves up to the front of the Brit-pop class with this classy follow-up. The pulse quickens on *Blood*, a diverse yet cohesive batch of graceful pop tunes that reveals growing confidence and discipline."

People: "Coldplay creates moments of absolute poetry on *Blood*, blending moody guitars and bass, subtle percussion and emphatic keyboards on tightly wrought dissections of political and personal disasters. Their pain is pure listening pleasure."

Entertainment Weekly: "Displaying a cohesion rarely heard in albums these days, *Blood* bobs from one majestic high to another. It's a relief to hear music that revels in the joys of simple, graceful melody."

Blender: "This album marks a band maturing into greatness. The sounds on *Blood* are simultaneously terse and expansive—moody and powerful, shot through with Chris Martin's grainy delivery. His voice is Coldplay's trump card; conveying real soulfulness rather than callow deliberation. The competition must now be wetting itself."

Stuff: "Coldplay has delivered a masterpiece."

Time Out New York: "The genius of Coldplay songs is the way they worm their way into the listeners' feelings of melancholy, reverie, and love. The songs graft themselves onto those emotions so that your own personal bullshit feels cinematic and large. If Coldplay hasn't gotten you yet, just give it a few months. You're bound to be due for a good, healthy cry sooner or later."

Calls and e-mails were now flooding into my office from industry executives and top radio programmers hailing the advance of *A Rush of Blood*. Advance copies minus artwork were sent out to generate industry excitement with a simple handwritten note, saying, "C-Ya at the Grammys." The word of mouth was what record labels can only dream of and pretty soon *A Rush of Blood* became the record everyone *had* to have as everyone seemed to pick different songs as their own personal favorite. It rapidly became the industry record of choice as burned copies were being passed around from one label employee to the next. In an e-mail sent to me, KROQ's Gene Sandbloom wrote, "Wow . . . what a stunner. Such growth from *Parachutes*. How they have matured in just one

album. From 'Politix' to 'Amsterdam,' this is truly an achievement."

With "In My Place" entrenched at several radio formats, as well as MTV, MTV2, and VH1, Coldplay was armed and ready to take on America and the fast-food mentality of the disposable pop machine. "I'm up for the challenge of trying to get passionate music into the mainstream. Our goal is to change the mainstream. We don't want to just keep ourselves a secret. We want to fight to have sincere music be the main thing again. That's why I'm so pleased to see U2 and Springsteen and even Dave Matthews out there. It's cool because they're all writing heartfelt stuff. And right now they'll rival anyone at the top. They, and right before them Eminem, are all doing passionate stuff and we just want to be a part of that," explained Martin. During their first interview in America for *A Rush of Blood* with, once again, KCRW's Nic Harcourt, Martin also stated, "It's sad that the surface view you get of America is the packaged microwaved pop when there is such amazing art that comes out of America. Tom Waits, the Flaming Lips, the Cohen brothers . . . there's inspiration all around. We want more soul into the mainstream and we are all for helping." But as we have come to know, with Chris Martin, the spirit and the confidence also comes with the contradiction, the other side of the coin. "At the moment, I am personally scared beyond all belief that we might be no more than a one-hit wonder. This interview right now might be the last promotional request we ever get." With that, laughter erupted from Harcourt and radio station employees, but not a peep from Martin, who nervously rubbed his head in a fit of visible worry. Harcourt could only reply with, "Come on, Chris. This album is brilliant.

Other major market stations began joining the ranks, and soon the band, management, and label had quite the dilemma on their hands. It was a known fact that the general feeling was "The Scientist" was going to be next up from the album. Fearing that Coldplay was soon to become a multiformat pop band for the masses, both KROQ and WBCN wanted to play something from the band that was more keyed up and edgy than a ballad, thus discovering "Clocks" by themselves. "When we got the full album, we knew it was deep; but 'Clocks' is just genius. We wanted to get that one on as soon as possible," states KROQ music director Lisa Worden. Adds program director of WBCN Oedipus, "I had no idea what the next single was going to be. I just loved it and wanted to play it. 'Clocks' grabbed me from the first time I heard the opening piano line."

With that, agendas were shifted, and just like "Trouble" before it, "Clocks" took on a life of its own. Once those two stations came in and began having immediate success with the song, radio stations began to fall like dominoes. One after another, from East Coast to West and in between, all jumped to "Clocks." The tune peaked at number 9 on the modern rock chart, making it the second-highest-charting single for the band next to "Yellow." In the end, the instincts of KROQ, WBCN and the handful of early believers were dead on as "Clocks" garnered the ultimate honor a song could receive by nabbing the 2004 Grammy Award for "record of the Year." Quite the underdog victory as "Clocks" took the statue over more established mainstream hits such as Eminem's "Lose Yourself," Outkast's "Hey Ya!" and Beyoncé Knowles's "Crazy in Love."

As much as awards are utter nonsense, it's cool to win them.

[Chris Martin]

This early fall tour included a stop in Las Vegas where, once again, music industry guests were flown in for a weekend of Sin City fun that coincided with a sold-out Coldplay show at the Joint, inside the Hard Rock Hotel. Coldplay could do no wrong that night; this topnotch evening included Wil and Guy winning some extra per diem money at the blackjack tables and Chris dedicating their performance of "Clocks" to a stunned and glowing Lisa Worden. The band's live performances were now burgeoning and their intensity, their confidence, and their overall presentation were blossoming with each show. Next stop was the Greek Theater in the Hollywood Hills and this was Coldplay's largest headline show in America to date. Martin was in fine form, calling this show "the closest thing we have to a homecoming in America" as they launched into an inspired version of "God Put a Smile Upon Your Face." Coldplay was up to the task for this marquee show, *Rolling Stone* reported, "Layered with the subtle slide work of guitarist Buckland, and lead singer Martin's delicate, searing falsetto, the songs managed to sound both elegant and raw. Surprisingly, they were also kind of fun."

As the band made their way around the country, I caught up with them in the eastern part of the U.S. for two shows in Boston and New York. They were invited to be the guests of honor at Oedipus's home for an aftershow party. As they could have easily started saying no to the countless promotional requests that were being shoved at them,

Coldplay played it smart, knowing their time to conquer was the present and they accepted the invitation. With a gorgeous house filled with radio station employees and friends, Oedipus pulled out all the stops, including a catered gourmet dinner with full bar. There was also a band meet and greet with his pet wolf, Contessa.

After the photo ops with the well-behaved wolf and drooling over Oedipus's unbeatable record collection, the next stop was Jones Beach, where once again self-doubt and dread came over Martin. "Why did you book us in this huge place?" Martin asked Dave Holmes. "I mean, this place is for, like, Britney Spears and Ozzy Osbourne. We're going to be playing for the janitors and beer vendors, man." Holmes, knowing his front man all too well, just shook his head and smiled. "Chris, relax . . . we sold over nine thousand tickets. It will look great tonight." When told that capacity was near 12,000, Martin went on a promotional rampage, agreeing to do a radio station visit with WLIR-FM in Long Island, a phone-in to WXRK New York, a press interview with a local Internet fanzine, and an MTV2 interview. Martin, working on pure adrenaline, was able to complete all this in under an hour. During the WLIR-FM interview, Gary Cee, the on-air DJ, said there were "Just a few tickets left; so hurry on down to Jones Beach." Martin sarcastically chimed in, "Yeah . . . come on down if you want to run around and stretch your legs out." The *only* thing Martin complained about during this promotional boot camp was the white limousine that was ordered to take us from the radio station to Jones Beach. "Do me a favor," Martin said seriously, looking at both Dave Holmes and myself, "no more fucking limousines. Why couldn't we have just rode here in a van or something? I bloody hate these things," as he looked around the stretch limo with its shameless and gaudy interior. Chris Martin had become a promotional wizard, a one-man machine; it was a planet's distance from where he was with all this just two years ago and it was impressive. In a span of ten minutes, Martin was seen holding a cell phone talking to a DJ from WXRK, while being interviewed on MTV2, taking questions from a reporter, then rushing back to the stage for Coldplay's concurrent soundcheck. Martin didn't let up until the house lights went down and walked on to the stage to see a completely filled Jones Beach Amphitheater. What I experienced that night, from the lights to the sound to the stage setup to the set list to the backdrop of the Atlantic Ocean that surrounded the Jones Beach Amphitheater and everything else about the band's overall performance, was a band that had fully arrived. I remember that the word that kept coming to my mind throughout that night was "complete." Coldplay had become the complete package. *Entertainment Weekly* was on hand to review and said, "It was the evening of September 19 and it was the lovefest that was Coldplay's show under the stars at New York's Jones Beach. It was the band's largest headlining gig ever. They

delivered a corking good set, played a grab bag assortment of great tunes, and have now established themselves as bona fide stateside rock stars." After the show, an exhausted but glowing Martin glided over to me and said, "Man, after what we did today I feel like a porn star who just spent twelve hours in front of the camera."

"Slowly breaking through the daylight."
—"Daylight"

Coldplay came back to the States in December, as they did the previous year, to hit the major markets for a run of radio station-sponsored Christmas shows. This time, though, they were returning as headliners. "Clocks" was receiving major video airplay and jamming at modern rock and adult contemporary. It broke the record for largest numbers of spins ever (in any given week) at the AAA format. Usually dedicated to more "upper-demo" artists like Sarah McLachlan and Bonnie Raitt, this format, which stands for adult album alternative, became yet another home for the band. The modern rock Christmas shows had become tailored around Coldplay's worldwide traveling schedule and they had now become *the* main marquee attraction. These shows included KROQ Los Angeles, WBCB Boston, WXRK New York, WHFS Washington, D.C., and a closing show with WPLY Philadelphia. The tour couldn't have kicked off any better with a show-stealing performance at the KROQ show on December 7th. Though they were billed as the headliner, Coldplay was put on second to last, sandwiched between Beck and multiplatinum arena rockers Creed. Creed insisted that they close the show. They couldn't have made a more colossal mistake. The night clearly belonged

to Coldplay. First, Beck hand-picked Chris Martin to sing a duet of the eighties Bob Geldof-penned charity classic "Feed the World." Martin innocently strolled out on stage for Beck's planned encore and immediately the 6,000-plus crowd got up from their seats for a standing ovation. Second, during the band's set, a frantic and overzealous Robert Hilburn of the *L.A. Times* rushed over to our row of seats that included program director Kevin Weatherly and shouted in Weatherly's ear, "Coldplay is now your most important band. This is their moment." Third, and what was clearly a dagger to the heart, during Creed's opening number, lead singer Scott Stapp's microphone went out, causing the already tense band to stop their set. As Creed stormed off the stage in a huff, the sold-out crowd began a deafening chant of "Coldplay, Coldplay, Coldplay." Two years, almost to the day, Coldplay walked on the same exact KROQ stage as a wound-up and somewhat uneasy English pop band. But on this night two storybook years later, Coldplay had emerged as conquering idols and megastars. On the remainder of the Christmas run, the energy

didn't subside. At the WXRK New York show at Nassau Coliseum, Coldplay went toe-to-toe with this century's first supergroup, Audioslave (made up of Soundgarden's Chris Cornell and three members of Rage Against the Machine), as the two bands easily came up as the big winners of the station's eight-band lineup. In Washington, D.C., the RIAA (the organization that oversees and tracks album sales) planned for a quaint gathering backstage to award the band with a certified platinum plaque for *A Rush of Blood to the Head*. When the guys entered the room, cameras lit up and a pack of adoring girls made a mad dash toward the band. When Martin extended his hand to greet them, one of the fans simultaneously broke into tears; true Coldplaymania in its most natural form. After headlining WPLY's show at the 15,000-seat US Air Arena in Philadelphia, Coldplay concluded 2002 in America with another return performance on CBS's *The Late Show with David Letterman*. Much deserved time off was in order for the boys as the year 2003 was primed and set up to be the band's most significant and unequaled year to date.

Chapter 16

"Tigers Waiting to Be Tamed"

As they did in 2001 and 2002, Coldplay kicked off the new year with another American tour. This tour, unlike the previous that would cover only the major markets of the country, was to hit American cities where the band had yet to play, places such as Charlotte, Dallas, Houston, Austin, St. Louis, Kansas City, Salt Lake City, Phoenix, Orlando, and the opening date on the tour, Miami. In the nearly three years of playing the States, the band had never made it to Florida; Miami was in the cards on the very first tour back in February of 2001, but it was one of the handful that had to be canceled after Martin's voice went out in New York City. With *A Rush of Blood* well over platinum and selling over 40,000 copies a week in America alone, Miami Beach, during the height of a cold January winter, was not a bad place to begin a tour.

Not taking anything for granted, Coldplay's itinerary was chockfull of promotional events. At Miami's radio station WZTA on the day of their show, Martin and Buckland dropped by the station for a live interview and performance in front of an in-studio audience. When asked if all the promotional engagements and constant touring gets to the band, Martin's answer was, "This is a great job, you know. Occasionally, we all have people that we miss and that we want to see, but none of us want to be working in a mine or digging ditches. Isn't it amazing we can come to a place that is, like, six thousand miles from where we live, and just do this as a job?" The band's frame of mind had now clearly settled into a comfortable place of supreme confidence and ease. They'd finally grown

accustomed to touring, to living out of suitcases. Instead of fighting the rigorous lifestyle—one city after another, one hotel after the next, and one look-a-like concert hall after another (and getting larger with each tour)—the band embraced it. They took to road life with full force, but as they do with everything, they were able to do this of their own volition. Martin was now able to have his own tour bus. This was not out of some pompous desire or newfound case of wanting to be the next Axl Rose, but rather out of necessity. Coldplay's traveling rock 'n' roll circus now consisted of three luxury-line tour buses: one for the crew, the second for Wil, Jonny, Guy, their in-house DJ, Wayne, and their new personal trainer and head of security, Rocky; the third was for Martin and whoever wanted a good and sane night's rest. The second bus was now the "party bus," the bus to hang in if you wanted to drink, smoke, listen to music, or challenge Wil to a game of Sega Basketball in the back room. Martin needed his own bus to protect his mind, health, body and most important his *voice*. Coldplay learned the hard way, back in the winter of 2001, that if they were to become the world's biggest rock band that they would need to take care of themselves. This was a priority to the band and all four now worked out every morning with Rocky and hotels that were booked in advance had to have a top-notch gym and workout room. Though tame and comparably innocent, aftershow boozing was commonplace and it seemed to actually help keep the band and their crew fresh and vibrant as the tours carried on. "We always seem to be on tour here, in the States, and it's real hardcore. Every time we come over here we think we're like Bono and the new U2, but we swiftly get reminded that we still have loads to prove. We love coming here, but it's a challenge," said Martin during the WZTA interview. Martin and Buckland closed this particular session with an acoustic version of "The Scientist" by saying, "This is perhaps the most beautiful song we will have ever written. Some songs just sort of arrive and you just can't believe you got 'em." With that, they launched into a memory-making version of what was to be the follow-up single to "Clocks."

The winter tour of 2003 marched on and the band seemed to be picking up steam with each city. During this leg, the 2002 Grammy Awards were announced and, like its UK counterpart the Brit Awards, Coldplay was once again nominated for Alternative Album of the Year. They also picked up a second nomination for Best Rock Song Performed by a Group for "In My Place." They ended up winning the Brit Awards' two highest honors of Best British Album and Best British Group. It was Coldplay's acceptance speech that plastered the band all over newspapers in every part of the world the following day: "Awards are all essentially nonsense and we're all going to die when George Bush has his way. But it will be great to go out with a bang," Martin barked out from the podium. It was meant in jest, but because of the all the success they were experiencing around the world, everything that Martin now said in public was scrutinized.

Like it or not, he had become a "spokesperson" for the new generation. Fans, younger bands, teenagers, and college students looking for a messiah, and of course the press hounds, were turning to Coldplay, and its charismatic lead singer, to get their views and opinions on world issues and global concerns.

War on terrorism and an invasion of Iraq was imminent and everyone wanted to know what Coldplay thought about it. In conjunction with Oxfam, Martin and the band had become leaders in the fight for international fair trade, causing the press to view Coldplay as liberal rebels for justice. Maketradefair.com was just an appetizer, a teaser, and now "they" wanted more from the band. There was a gaping hole for an outspoken and intelligent rock celebrity and Chris Martin fit the bill. Educated, intelligent, witty, charming, humble, and good-looking were the qualifications and though Martin was a match, it was quickly and unanimously agreed among the boys that, following the 2003 Brit Awards episode, "less is more" would be the words to live by and it would be more beneficial to everyone involved if they let their music do the talking.

The Grammy Awards Committee (NARM), knowing how hot Coldplay had become, booked the band to perform live at the awards show on February 9th at Madison Square Garden. This performance would be shown live on CBS and have a viewing audience in excess of 25 million. Always one to throw a curveball, Coldplay boldly picked the lead track off the album, "Politix," and arranged for the New York Philharmonic to be the backing orchestra. "It really seemed like the only appropriate song to play," says Champion. "It's the song that's able to say everything for us. We're on our way to war, the Grammys are in New York City . . . it's the only song we felt right about playing." With New York City as the host site, and the impending battle in the Middle East as backdrop, Coldplay put every ounce of guts and urgency into their performance and the emotion and intensity shined through.

"Politix" was easily one of the show's highlights and it stood right next to memorable performances from Eminem (backed by the Roots), Simon and Garfunkel's first public performance in over ten years, and a powerful Clash tribute that featured Bruce Springsteen, Dave Grohl, and Elvis Costello. "Politix," with the New York Philharmonic adding the extra punch, was so gorgeous that picking up two awards in both categories of Alternative Album and Rock Song was merely an afterthought. This was Coldplay's night indeed, but if you were with the band you would have hardly known it.

"As far as the Grammys, we went in, played, and left. We don't like doing red carpets . . . that's a load of nonsense. I think Wil saw Dave Grohl and we stood next to Aretha Franklin for a moment, but that was it," Martin told radio station 99X in Atlanta. He added, "We honestly don't care about that stuff. It's complete bollocks. Celebrities are just regular people with worse childhoods."

Directly after the Grammys, back home in England, all four attended the annual NME Carling Awards. Far from just another awards show, the NME Carling Awards is an unrestricted, casual affair. Bands are rarely seen without a drink or smoke in their hands and it seems the more oblique and more repugnant the acceptance speech the better. A relaxed and upbeat Coldplay took the high road as the band scored big, winning Album of the Year for *A Rush of Blood*. Asked by *NME* how it felt to win, Martin said, "It's amazing. As I said on-stage that we could have gone into Shania Twain territory,

now being a big band, so to get *NME* and *NME* readers still thinking we're cool is brilliant. It's amazing. I can't believe we won this."

On March 6th their tour landed the band back in Atlanta to play in front of over 10,000 people. They actually had the afternoon free, a rarity on this engagement-filled run, and gladly accepted an invitation to spend the day with pop music icon and Atlanta resident Sir Elton John. Remembers manager Holmes, "Because of 9/11 and a freakish rainstorm that caused us to cancel an August show, we hadn't played a proper gig in Atlanta since early 2001. The guys wanted to do something special for this particular show." Chimes in Berryman, "Elton got a hold of us and invited us over for lunch at his home. He had this huge loft in downtown Atlanta. It looked like he bought an entire floor of this building and knocked down the walls and turned it into this gargantuan one-story mansion. It seemed endless, with great artwork on every wall and just one piano in the middle of it all." Martin also fondly recalls this visit. "So I just asked him, 'Do you want to play a song with us tonight at our show?,' thinking nothing of it really. His eyes lit up and we decided on 'Trouble.' I just sat down on the one piano he had and started teaching him the song." "It was mad. Here we were showing Elton John, of all people, how to play one of our songs. Mind-blowing," adds Champion. Martin continues, "Like, less than two minutes into showing him . . . he stopped me and said, 'I got it. I got it. If I need to, I'll listen to the album. I have it somewhere.' Absolutely brilliant."

At the concert, Rocky, Coldplay's head of security, remembers some backstage jitters coming from Sir

Elton's dressing room. "He kept going back to this little room backstage that had a keyboard so he could rehearse the song by himself. He was quite nervous and it was touching how nervous he actually was. I even saw his hands trembling a little at the start of the song, but of course he played it perfectly. It was tremendous." Program director of 99X Leslie Fram was in the crowd when Coldplay's surprise guest walked onstage to join the band. "I had never heard a crowd erupt like that before.

It was ear-shattering. And Elton nailed it. It was breathtaking. It was like Elton and Coldplay had rehearsed it for weeks," claims Fram. On March 7th, the next day, Elton John called into 99X. "He called me on our morning show and told everyone how great the band was and how much he loved their music. That show and that version of 'Trouble' with Elton, just took Coldplay to yet another level. That moment was all anyone in Atlanta would talk about for days after," said Fram.

Chapter 17

"It's Not Rocket Scientist"

Though it is the premier ballad from the album, "The Scientist" sure didn't act like a typical slow-tempo number. Standard ballads normally take months to get steam rolling on the charts, but the song was already pumping on the modern rock Top 40 by the time Capitol Records released the single to radio stations in April 2003. The accompanying video for the track served as the decisive payoff pitch. Shot atypically in reverse time, Chris Martin actually had to learn how to sing the song backwards. "It took a long time. I had the biggest sheets of paper with the weirdest words on it. From Las Vegas to San Diego I had to learn a new language. It was like I just took a crash course in backwards lip-synching," says Martin. The video, a heart-wrenching tale of a couple driving a black sedan over a cliff in the English countryside, features a standout performance by Martin as he tells the sad tale through the power of the song's lyrics. The video was immediately added to the MTV and VH1 playlists and, once again, another Coldplay treasure was well on its way.

I joined up with the band during the final two shows of their American winter tour. On Wednesday, March 12th in snow-covered Milwaukee, the band's mood was one of comfort and tranquility. Their backstage room at Eagles Ballroom suited their aura as they now seemed at ease with their stardom. Coldplay's restricted area included a pinball machine, two video games, couches, Indian rugs, a healthy spread of fruits, vegetables, cheeses, and imported beer, along with fresh plants covered in Christmas lights. Part of the casual vibe that had been created was also due to the fact that this, and the following evening's show in Minneapolis, was to be the band's last in the States until the summer. A conversation broke out about how things had become noticeably different back home for each member. Over the previous couple of years, the occasional fan or autograph hound would spot one of the guys during a rare break in recording or touring. This simple fame had now evolved into the cold, hard fact that anyone with a camera and ties to a slimy tabloid were sure to be hanging out at the boys' doorsteps. "I don't mind being recognized by neighbors and fans or whatever; it's just the paparazzi trying to take a picture of me while I'm out jogging or coming out of my door to get lunch or something. Like, who cares? It's such a waste," says Martin. There was talk of personal bodyguards but, like disapproving of riding in limousines and other rock 'n' roll clichés, Martin and the rest would have none of that talk.

It was on this tour that Coldplay introduced a couple of new songs into their arsenal. A vintage midtempo Coldplay style piece, "Ladder to the Sun," and an out-of-the-ordinary rocker, "Poor Me." Sonically reminiscent of a B-side off the "In My Place" single called "The One I Love," the latter is proof that Coldplay refuses to rest on their "meal ticket sound" and the boys continue to outdo themselves and mature in more than one musical avenue. "Poor Me" is and will be an undeniable rock radio smash. Both haunting musically and lyrically, the song continues Martin's theme of living in the moment and not blowing any opportunities bestowed upon you.

"Poor me, I'm floating out to sea. An opportunity that went by. Poor you, oh what you gonna do? No what you gonna do, you just cry. I hear ya, come nearer. I hear ya, but I don't understand."

"Ladder to the Sun" also captures the spirit of seeking out one's fate and owning one's own destiny. "This song is about grabbing opportunity with both hands," said Martin, as he passionately clenches his two hands to introduce the new tune, to the appreciative sold-out Milwaukee audience. Having never played these new markets before, it was clearly apparent the pure power that radio airplay still has in this country. Though every song during the nearly two-hour set was met with glee and admiration, it was the radio hits "Yellow," "Trouble," and especially their new anthems "Clocks" and "The Scientist" that received the evening's largest decibel levels. At the Target Center in Minneapolis, home of the Minnesota Timberwolves, Martin introduced "Trouble" by saying, "This is a sad song. A sad song for a fun night." After "In My Place," the band's second encore, in a moment of genuine emotion and confident wit, Martin looked around his own stage and said, "Thank you, Jonny, thank you, Paul, Ringo, and George." With the MAKETRADEFAIR sign glaring bright behind them, the band put their arms around one another and bowed in perfect Beatles synch to their adoring audience. Another show in the books, another city dominated, and another over-the-top tour a smashing success, Coldplay now appeared invincible. Invincible, unconquerable, and unbeatable, Coldplay had reached this level by defying the rules, thrashing the odds against them, flogging their doubters, and doing so on their own terms. As soon as the house lights dimmed, the four would have the crowd eating out of the palms of their hands.

Over the next two hours, at every stop on this tour, the audience would be mesmerized, standing on every word coming from Martin's mouth.

I met up with the band just two days before their Hollywood Bowl shows, on May 28th, in California's capital city, Sacramento. Maybe it was the fact that it was only their second show of this all-important trek around America's biggest venues or maybe it was the fact that the temperature was sitting at a steamy 100 degrees when the band arrived at the Sleep Train Amphitheater, some fifty rice patty-filled miles north of Sacramento. Maybe it was the combination of the two, but the fact remained that there was clear and visible tension in the Coldplay ranks. To add some frosting to this cake, it was also the amphitheater's first concert of the season and the venue was experiencing some technical difficulty with Coldplay's four megascreens, used as the backdrop to the band's performance. Conversations between band and crew were quick and to the point and small talk was kept to a minimum. The Coldplay "corporation" took on even more of a big red machine appearance with their bodyguard and security count now doubled and the type of laminates and VIP sticky passes for band access having tripled. Martin came to the venue with a full head of hair and a beard reminiscent of a late-sixties Paul McCartney or Jim Morrison. The others also had facial hair and were tanned with toned bodies. When Martin hit the stage for their staple opening number, 'Politix,' his hair was all but gone and his full beard was now cleaned to a nice Don Johnson in *Miami Vice* stubble. But neither Martin's butchery of a hairdo or the muggy night, that felt like the bayou in August could break or weaken Coldplay as they ripped through an extraordinary ready-for-primetime set full of their hits, album cuts, and even two new songs, "Poor Me" (which was introduced on the band's last American tour), and a song inspired

by true infatuation called "Moses." It was the latter about which Martin joked during the introduction of the song, saying, "This new song goes out to the person who cut off all my hair backstage." "Moses," like "Poor Me," is destined to be a keeper in the growing Coldplay catalog. Obviously a writer in the throes of devotion, Martin uses the character of Moses as a metaphor for someone who has come along to save him and show him the light of love.

"Like Moses has power over the sea, so you've got power over me . . . You're air that I can breathe, 'cause you're my golden opportunity. Come on now, don't you wanna see? Just what a difference you've made in me."

The humility and then the humor didn't die off during the course of the evening. Still eager to take a self-effacing jab at "Trouble," Martin quipped, "Sorry if you guys out there thought you bought tickets to OzzFest [the metalfest, arriving at the amphitheater later that month, was being advertised on the venue's marquee just below Coldplay]. . . . Ozzy can surely make this song into a pop classic." As the show progressed the band still had an urgency about their performance, as if they still had something to prove. Capacity of the venues on this new tour was almost double in every market and while everyone in the lower sections were on their feet, Martin felt it a requirement to get *everyone* in attendance involved. During the beginning of "Yellow," Martin stormed around the stage and in his best impersonation of Bono, said, "Stand up. Please stand up. Everyone up. I'll tell you what . . . stand up and you get a prize. Come on." There was something sweetly innocent about his smile when the crowd acknowledged and granted him his wish

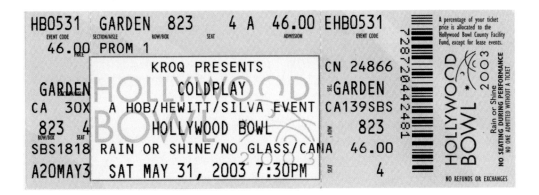

and especially sweet when the 18,000-plus audience sang along in unison to "Trouble," "Yellow," and "Everything's Not Lost." After the sing-along of *they spun a web for me*" in "Trouble," Martin looked up from his piano and gratefully said, "And what a great web you all have spun." Though the edginess and restlessness behind the scenes was clear, Coldplay and their arena-made ninety minutes of rock music were ready for the prestigious cathedral known as the Hollywood Bowl.

Saturday May 31st, 2003 was the first of two dates at the celebrated Hollywood Bowl. The 20,000-seat amphitheater, resting deep inside the Hollywood Hills, was overfilled and there must have been at least another thousand hiding in the hills and hanging in the tress that surround the Bowl. This is a concert site for the serious only; the Beatles, the Who, Bob Marley, and Radiohead are some of the few rock icons that have played the venue. Coldplay sold out not one but *two* nights here (Monday, June 2nd) and a third could have been easily accomplished if only the routing of the tour allowed it. During an interview with KROQ Los

Angeles DJ Stryker before the show, which was recorded live for a nationally syndicated radio audience, Martin remained humble about the band's rise into rock's elite. "There are times we do think we are invincible and the best; then I open up one of my girlfriends' magazines, like *Ms.*, and see they gave us two stars out of five or something . . . and that brings me right back down."

In an obvious and tactical move to play down to the Bowl's enormous stage size, Coldplay kept their set design to a bare minimum; this could only spark immediate references to "another" English band (okay . . . the Beatles) that graced the Bowl's stage in both 1964 and 1965 with their minimalist onstage approach. It was a stroke of pure credibility and cool as Coldplay once again would let their music do the talking. The show, on this early summer Saturday night, ran the gamut of emotions; the people lucky enough to get the hottest ticket in town were treated to it all. There were times during opening numbers such as "God Put a Smile Upon Your Face" and "Daylight" when the crowd in the Bowl felt as if rock 'n' roll once again had found its sense of purpose and the future of the music world was not all doom and gloom. There were also times where you could have heard a pin drop during songs such as "The Scientist" or "Amsterdam." There were even comedic undertones throughout the night, as Martin joked with his lyrics on "Everything's Not Lost," adding a section on the spot, *"And if you think you've got a bad haircut. You hope it might grow back one day. And hope that everything's not lost."* During "Trouble," Martin broke into a slick version of Nelly's "Hot in Here." And during a solo rendition of Louie Armstrong's "What a Wonderful World" it was easy to spot someone, guy or girl, wiping tears from their eyes. *L.A. Times* critic Robert Hilburn commented, "Martin, as did Armstrong, sings it with a purity and faith that makes you want to suspend disbelief and dream along." "What a Wonderful World" sparked an immediate standing ovation and sent Martin backstage to join the other three before they came back on for their encore.

It was at this point in the show, during the encore, when true euphoria and liberation came as the band went from "Clocks" right into a pulsating version of "In My Place." The Hollywood Bowl became as one and the band's performance of the song was nothing short of tribal. When Martin moved across the stage during the number, he didn't walk, he bopped. When he took off from one side of the floor to the other, he didn't jog, he jumped. The Bowl became his to own. The *L.A. Times* agreed, saying, "The image that remains the evening's strongest was the inspirational, communal embrace during the show's penultimate song, 'In My Place.' With the band and audience united in singing the refrain, it was a vision of rock

after the rapture." Yes, Coldplay had taken over the Hollywood Bowl, the city of Los Angeles, and the nation via a live radio broadcast from a Westwood One radio network satellite feed. The *L.A. Times* review of the show led with the headline of "With a Smoothness and Commitment to Principle Reminiscent of U2, the Likable Band Coldplay Touches Its Bowl Audience." Richard Cromelin's review went on to say, "Don't look now, but rock has a new candidate for canonization. Coldplay's Chris Martin seemed to be fitted for a halo." Once again, as it happened back in the summer of 2001 with their much-needed breakthrough Tabernacle show in Atlanta, the stiffness and the jitters that surrounded the band in Sacramento just three days prior seemed to have lifted. After a second triumphant night at the Bowl, the band would begin their drive, with major city and famous venue stops along the way, to New York City for their date with the Garden.

"Hello, we're Coldplay. Thanks for making our dreams come true," said Martin to the Madison Square Garden's 18,000 strong on Friday the 13th of June 2003.

The band launched into a chilling and unifying version of "God Put a Smile Upon Your Face," now the trademark second song of their set, and you can tell that this night was going to be one to remember. Leave it to the last show of their arena tour, the triumphant and long-awaited sold-out show in New York City, to be their best. "This is our last show of the tour and our last show in America for a long, long time," belted out Martin during the middle of the concert. The band was playing on the highest of levels and the crowd was right there along for the ride. This was Coldplay at its best. This was what the four friends, Chris, Jonny, Wil, and Guy, had aimed for all along, what they had set their sights on when they first met up at Ramsey Hall at UCL in 1996. But even the wildest of their fantasies never really matched what they were experiencing on this Friday night. Hard work, dedication, commitment, belief, passion, and ambition had paid off and Coldplay's dreams *had* come true. "If you're here to see Cher, that was last night," joked Martin as he played the opening notes to "The Scientist," the last song on their set list. The night that never wanted to end; Coldplay at Madison Square Garden. The first encore included "Clocks," "In My Place" (which never disappoints), and "Amsterdam." The band came roaring back for a second encore and treated the crowd (still not an empty seat in the house) to Echo and the Bunnymen's "Lips Like Sugar." If it wasn't for the mandatory, by the book, Garden-mandated union curfew, Coldplay could've played into the morning hours; the band appeared ready too and the adoring crowd appeared ready to watch the sun come up with their favorite band.

"Thanks for giving us this job," Martin said in his still-consistent humble manner to the standing ovation of 18,000 plus. And with that the house lights went up and a truly historic rock 'n' roll show was history. Coldplay's long American journey to the summit that had started all the way back in the fall of 2000 was now complete. Coldplay was now at their highest peak and conquering Madison Square Garden was truly a crowning moment, with many more encores to follow.

Conclusion

"The One I Love"

It was 10:30 P.M. PST when I checked my cell phone's voice mail to find I had one new message. "Hello . . . Gary . . . this is Chris. I'm really sorry to hear that you had lost your job. I think it's horrible. I'm here in Miami and we are starting our tour. It won't be the same without you, man. I'm just up watching movies and worrying that no one will show up for our show tomorrow night. Well, happy new year . . . I guess."

I decided to leave work early on Friday, January 4th, 2003. I had finished a mailing I had to do, cleared out all my e-mails, and returned all my calls. The office was dead; after all, the "real" first day for everyone to be back at work was supposed to be the following Monday. Executives were just getting back from whatever holiday season vacation they took and radio stations wouldn't begin reporting their playlists for the new year until the following week. So I did something I rarely, if ever, did; I told my assistant I was feeling ill and needed to go home for the day. I was about to play hooky. My wife and kids were at Disneyland (school for my son and daughter were to commence the following Monday), so I thought I'd take a drive to my neighborhood movie theater and catch a matinee. I was standing in line deciding which movie to choose when my cell phone rang. "Gary, hey . . . they want you back in the office right away." It was my assistant calling to tell me that I was needed in my boss's office ASAP. "What's up?" I said to him. "I dunno. They just said for you to get back because they need to see you right away. They need to see you in person," he replied.

I hung up the call, got out of the ticket line, and rushed back to my car. This is not good . . . not good at all, I thought to myself. I made just two phone calls on my way back to Capitol. One to my lawyer at the time, who was out for the day (gee, what a shocker), and one to my wife, who was currently in the heart of Disneyland waiting for the daily Main Street parade to begin. I told her something was wrong at work and I'd been asked to return. I remember telling her to expect the worst; it was the right phone call to make. As always, my wife was calm and levelheaded . . . I needed that.

As I parked my car at the Capitol lot and went up eight stories to the executive floor, I ran through all sorts of scenarios. What exactly did I screw up to have to come back to the office . . . on a Friday afternoon, no less? Just be ready to come up with answers. Be ready for anything, is what was racing through my mind. As I entered the executive office, there were three people waiting for me. The label's general manager, the head of Promotion, and the one person who I really didn't want to see, the label's head of Human Resources. It was the time of massive layoffs, consolidation, and merging and you knew it wasn't a good thing when the head of Human Resources was taking a meeting with you. So there I was with three people who I didn't want to be with. The meeting was short, crass, and just a little too formal. "We are going to make some changes in the department and . . . ahhh, we're gonna have to let you go," is how the meeting started. I don't care if I knew this was going to happen to me hours before, days before, or weeks before; nothing, I mean *nothing*, can pre-pare you for someone saying that you've just been fired. "Why?" was the only word I could muster. "We're just going in another direction" was the stock answer they kept coming back with. "You're a great guy, Gary. You did great work. We just need to go in a different direction." I gave the head of Human Resources a quick glance and I could tell she wanted no part of this. I did not envy her job. I knew this "meeting" was going nowhere fast and that any arguing or debating this decision would fall on deaf ears. I took the high road, stood up, looked around, and offered a sarcastic "happy new year" to the room and marched out. That was it . . . over and done. Close to five years of blood, sweat, and tears put into that place. Too many extra hours spent in the office, too many extra nights out seeing shitty live bands, too many extra days spent on the road promoting Capitol's artists, and for what? To have someone say on a Friday afternoon in January, "We're going in a different, direction we're gonna let you go"? I wish I could tell you why I was fired. Like I was caught running around the fourth floor naked, screaming," The Beatles are coming, the Beatles are coming." Or, more realistic, that I stole a truckload of CDs from the building and used it to pay my mortgage. Nothing like that. Nothing close to it. Unless you count "we're going to go in another direction" as a valid enough reason.

I was one of just three remaining vice presidents left from the previous regime. The one thing that had kept me at the label for so long was the love of the music and its roster, and easily at the top of the list for me was Coldplay. Just two days before the start of yet another Coldplay tour in the States

was when my services as a Capitol employee were no longer required. How dare they take away the one thing that was keeping me there in the first place, I thought; they can't really take Coldplay away from me, can they?

It seemed right that the first phone call I received from an artist on the label was from none other than Chris. That's just another example of why he and the band mean so much to people. Coldplay is a small, tightly wound, close-knit family. The perfect circle of Coldplay is based on trust, honesty, and loyalty. To get in with Coldplay is extremely difficult, but awfully simple to explain. Like any long-lasting and true friendship in life, you can't force or buy your way in. The same rules and regulations apply. I've worked with dozens upon dozens of bands before, in close and intimate quarters, and have had some unforgettable experiences with many and some forgettable, meaningless times with more than I care to mention. Coldplay was different. It's because of who they are as people and what they expect out of the people they trust; and it doesn't hurt that they make the most compelling and passionate music that this new century has heard. Maybe it's the way Chris, Jonny, Wil, and Guy were raised. Maybe it's how they've grown during their years as bandmates into four intellectual, humble, friendly, witty, and noncompromising individuals. Jonny, the calm and happy one. Guy, the honest but mysterious one. Wil, the proud and credible one. And Chris . . . the confident but self-effacing one; the humble but proud front man.

I looked at my watch, after I heard the message from Chris. 1:30 A.M. in Miami, I thought, there is *no* way he'll be up. What to do—what to do . . . I got it. I'll call back and leave a message on his voicemail. Coldplay's new American tour begins tomorrow night, I thought, so he'll probably call me back in the next couple of days. I dialed his cell and after one ring a very awake and chirpy voice on the other line said "hello." I was caught off guard, and like the mature husband and father of two that I am, I hung up. Great, just brilliant. I just hung up the phone on one of the single most engaging front men in all of rock music. Strong move, Gary. What to do—what to do. After a few seconds of going over my options, I realized I had no choice but to call him back. It's Martin's cell phone and I'm sure he has that "received calls" feature that can retrieve any call. So I pushed the redial button and once again, the same vibrant voice picked up, but this time the voice said, "Gary . . . is that you?" I put my tail between my legs and told him it was me who had just called.

After apologizing for hanging up on him and doing it the night before the beginning of his tour, Martin retorted by apologizing himself for calling so late. "Man, I forgot who I'm talking to . . . the king of the apology," I said. In just under an hour we covered so many topics; it was as if we were two war buddies who hadn't talked in months who needed to catch up with each other's lives. Martin thanked me for everything I did in helping out the band (yes, it was one of those sincere Chris Martin lines of "thanks a lot for everything that you did for us, man"), and I thanked him for making my job so worthwhile and for making such fabulous, uncompromising, and inspiring music. I closed the conversation by saying the one thing I'd regret the most about having to leave would be not getting to work with Coldplay anymore. Martin's answer is one that I will never forget. "Well, maybe we can find a way to still work together. Maybe it's in the stars."

Acknowledgments

I would first need to thank Chris Martin, Jonny Buckland, Guy Berryman, and Wil Champion for their "green light" to write this book. I wouldn't have even attempted to begin page one without their blessing and support to do so. To Dave Holmes, Coldplay's manager, who is the music industry's premier rock manager and a top-shelf human being. To my relentless lion of a manager and agent, Peter Miller. Without you this seriously would not be possible. To Jeff Kravitz for supplying this book with quality photographs and introducing me to Peter Miller. To Jacob Hoye for becoming my partner in bringing this dream of writing a book on the world's most important band to a reality. To David Altshuler for guiding me down the tricky road of legal affairs and to Nathan and Scott in Peter's office. Nathan, thanks for the kick in the pants and Scott, thanks for the continued faith. To Doris Spivack, for being the editing school-teacher/mother at which she is so good.

Also to the following who contributed to the book in more ways than one. Kevin Weatherly, Lisa Worden, Rodney Bingenheimer, and Gene Sandbloom at KROQ, Nic Harcourt and Ariana Morganstern at KCRW, Leslie Fram (who was first to step up for me) at 99X, Oedipus and Steven Strict at WBCN, Jim McGuinn and Dan Fein at Y100, Phil Manning at KNDD, Mark Hamilton at KNRK, Aaron Axelson at LIVE 105, Pat Ferrise and Bob Waugh at WHFS, Mike Peer at WXRK, Troy Hansen at WZTA, Bryan Schock at 91X, Mike Parrish at FMQB, Karen Glauber at *Hits* magazine, Gary Cee at WLIR-FM (yes, for more ways than one!), Chris Patyk, Blaze, Jennifer Waldburger, Estelle Wilkinson, Joe Rainey, DeeDee Kearney, Ryan Chester, Ricky Riker, Steve Nice, Dana White, Del Williams, Ty Braswell, Leah Simon, Jonathan McHugh (six degrees of Q), and Jed Weitzman.

Finally, and just as important as all above, to my wife, Jill Spivack, and my two children, Jake and Emma, for showering me with complete support and belief in going for it.

This unauthorized inside story was green-lighted by the members of Coldplay. Thank you for your blessing.

About the Author

Gary Spivack is a fourteen-year veteran of the music business. Over the last two decades, Gary has worked in the Promotion and Marketing Departments of Elektra Records, Atlantic Records, and Capitol Records and is currently a national promotion director at Geffen Records in Los Angeles, California. His experience has led him to travel across America promoting rock bands and building relationships with radio stations, booking agents, and club owners all over the country.

Gary resides in Pacific Palisades, California, with his wife, Jill, and his two kids, Jake and Emma.